Governance at Community Level in China and India

About the Authors

Prof. G. Palanithurai, Rajiv Gandhi Chair for Panchayati Raj Studies, and Dean, Students Welfare, Gandhigram Rural Institute, Gandhigram is an academic activist. He is specializing in grassroots governance and development. He closely works with local, regional and federal governments. He actively collaborates with civil society activities to strengthen Panchayati Raj System in India. He has developed a leadership school in Rajiv Gandhi Chair. To his credit he has sixty five books, eighty three monographs, seventy six popular articles, one hundred and thirty nine research articles in his area of specialization. He is a visiting professor in Cologne University, Germany. He extensively travelled abroad in academic assignments. His action research activities were supported by the Ford Foundation, the Population Foundation of India, DANIDA, Rajiv Gandhi Foundation, UNDP, The Hunger Project, UNICEF, The World Bank, State Planning Commission, Action Aid International, Swiss Development and Cooperation, Toolkit Foundation Netherland and a few other agencies. He is the coordinator of the UGC Sponsored Innovative Programme and UGC Special Assistance Programme of the Department of Political Science and Development Administration, Gandhigram Rural Institute.

Mr. Niclas D. Weimar is teaching assistant in the Department of Indology, Cologne University, Germany. He is consultant to many organizations for Solar Energy. He has to his credit four research articles and three books. He is pursuing research in Cologne University, Germany.

Thirumeni, B.S., who is working as a Joint Development Commissioner at the Rural Development Department, Kerala. Now he is dealing with Mahatma Gandhi NREGA. He is graduated in politics (Kerala University) and International Relations (Gandhiji University). He has got UGC Junior Research Fellow. Now he is doing PhD (part time) at the Gandhigram Rural University, Dindigul under the guidance of Dr. G. Palanithurai.

Governance at Community Level in China and India

A Comparative Analysis

G. PALANITHURAI
NICLAS D. WEIMAR
B. S. THIRUMENI

CONCEPT PUBLISHING COMPANY PVT. LTD.
NEW DELHI-110059

ISBN-13 : 978-93-5125-012-8

First Published 2014

Published and Printed by

Concept Since 1974

Concept Publishing Company Pvt. Ltd.
A/15-16, Commercial Block, Mohan Garden
New Delhi-110059 (India)
T: 25351460, 25351794, *F*: 091-11-25357109
E: publishing@conceptpub.com, W: www.conceptpub.com
Editorial Office: H-13, Bali Nagar, New Delhi-110 015, India.

Cataloging in Publication Data--*Courtesy:* D.K. Agencies (P) Ltd. <docinfo@dkagencies.com>

Palanithurai, G. (Ganapathy)
Governance at community level in China and India : a comparative analysis / G. Palanithurai, Niclas D. Weimar, B.S. Thirumeni.
p. cm.
Includes bibliographical references and index.
ISBN 9789351250128

1. Local government—China—Jiangsu Sheng. 2. Panchayat—India—Kerala. I. Weimar, Niclas D., joint author. II. Thirumeni, B. S., joint author. III. Title.

DDC 320.80951 23

To
The Divine Mother

Preface

Decentralization has to empower the citizens, build capacity of the people, decide priorities of the local needs and make the local populace to participate in the decision making process. Ultimately it has to fix certain responsibilities on them to decide many of the issues which affect their life. The new dispensation of decentralization of powers makes the communities to assume as much as responsibilities from the state and by which their status of beneficiaries or petitioners has to be changed as participants. Further, the whole process of development has to take place through a process of democratization.

Decentralization has its own weaknesses and yet the context and conditions demand decentralization. Decentralization will deliver goods if the institutions and the representatives involved in the activities of the institutions are empowered. Empowerment of institutions and representatives involved in decision making depends on many factors and of them the design of the institution, powers devolved to them, functionaries assigned to them finances devolved to them and support structure created are imperative requirements. Apart from the above, the level of awareness of the stakeholders about the process of governance and development is yet another factor which determines the effectiveness of decentralization of powers. Against this background ethnographic studies have been conducted at the grassroot level in two countries as to what extent the local governance institutions have been designed and how they are equipped with power and authority, are being studied. One lowest unit of rural local governance has been selected from China and India for an in-depth analysis. One village Panchayat from Kerala State has been selected from India and in the same way one village has been selected from Jiangsu province of China for this study. By comparing the two lowest units of governance in the two countries, the study has brought to light the significance of empowerment of the institutions for the effective delivery of services. It is to be noted here that one unit is from a liberal democratic country and another one is from the state regulated democratic country. There is yet another interesting feature one can notice in India and China. No doubt India is a democratic country but one cannot say that Indian society is fully oriented in democracy. In India we find democracy in institutional structures but in behaviour one could notice the authoritarian behaviour. In China it is a state regulated society and yet democratic practices are entertained. Through this study one can see the behaviour of the people at a community level towards governance, development and administration.

For a broader understanding of the students, both case studies have been compiled in a comparative perspective. Since comparable factors are in both countries socio-economic settings this attempt has been made. The prime aim of this monograph is to highlight how "will of the state" is more important in strengthening the grassroots institutions through this process of decentralization. Though decentralization is a world phenomenon, the whole process is top down. Since it is a top down process political will plays a predominant role.

"Social will" is also an imperative need for strengthening grassroots governance. But it is a bottom up process. The question have is whether the state is a facilitator or a dictator, whether the weight of the state is on the shoulders of the people or an instrument to reduce the burden of the people. These are the broader questions to be answered while analyzing the grassroots institutions.

Acknowledgements

When I was in Germany for a semester as visiting professor in Cologne University for a teaching assignment I was assisted by Mr. Niclas D. Weimar from the Indology Department. During my interaction with Niclas D. Weimar I found in him rare qualities of a researcher. I have given some assignments pertinent to local body institutions in Germany and he has completed the same to my satisfaction. Having seen his commitment in research I asked him to undertake a field work in China as he planned to visit China for a research project. He has agreed to do so. I have developed a very simple framework and I asked him to conduct this study in one village Panchayat in China. He has evinced keen interest in this work apart from his project work because of his deep desire to specialise in rural development issues. He has carried out the survey in a village Panchayat in China. As a result he brought a report based on the framework which I have given to him.

I have given the same framework to Mr. B.S. Thirumeni, my research scholar and asked him to conduct a study in Kerala village Panchayat. Based on his field work he brought out a small report. Both reports have been analysed and presented in the form of a small monograph. The purpose of this monograph is very simple. Since our students, who are undergoing course on decentralization, want to know comparatively the picture of local governance in a state regulated democracy, I made an attempt. I must thank both Mr. Niclas Weimar of Cologne University and my research scholar Mr. B.S. Thirumeni for their painstaking efforts to conduct the study as per my direction. Along with them I have to thank my faculty members and faculty members of Indology Department of Cologne University for their cooperation and support for my academic pursuits. My family members deserve my appreciation as they allow me to concentrate on my academic works without any demand from me. Finally, Mr. Ashok Kumar Mittal of Concept Publishing Company Pvt. Ltd. deserves special thanks as he with a single handed devotion is publishing large number of books on rural studies based on the field work done by the scholars. Concept Publishing Company has emerged as a specialized company publishing books on grassroots institution. Here I have to mention an event which took place long back in Delhi. I was in an international book fair looking for Books on decentralized governance in Sage stall. Mr. Tajeswar Singh of Sage asked me "what books you are searching here?". I said, "Decentralized governance". He said "This is not the right place and go and see in Concept Publishing Company stall you can get it". Now this company has emerged successful as a specialist in rural studies. He and his team deserve my appreciation.

Gandhigram
15.05.2012

G. Palanithurai

Contents

List of Tables, Figures and Photographs

Tables

Figures

Photographs

Abbreviations

ADS	Area Development Society
AL	Agricultural Labour
APC	Agricultural Producers' Cooperative
BJP	Bharatiya Janata Party
CCP	Chinese Communist Party
CDS	Community Development Society
CPI	Communist Party of India
CPI(M)	Communist Party of India (Marxist)
CT	Construction
DPC	District Planning Committee
GLF	Great Leap Forward
GMD	Guomindang
HRS	Household Responsibility System
ICDP	Integrated Child Development Programme
ICDS	Integrated Cattle Development Scheme
IRTC	Integrated Rural Technology Centre
ITI	Industrial Training Institute
JMS	Junior Middle School
JSLE	Jiangsu Province Election Legislation
JSZ	Jiangsu-Shanghai-Zhejiang
LFP	Livestock, Forestry, Fishing and Plantation Activities
LPG	Liquid Petroleum Gas
M&Q	Mining and Quarrying
MAT	Mutual-Aid Teams
MGNREGA	Mahatma Gandhi National Rural Employment Guarantee Act
MPSH	Manufacturing, Processing, Servicing and Repairs in Household Industries

MPSOH	Manufacturing, Processing, Servicing and Repairs in Other than Household Industries
NABARD	National Bank for Agriculture and Rural Development
NGO	Non Governmental Organisation
NHG	Neighbour Hood Group
NPC	National People's Congress
OBC	Other Backward Communities
OECD	Organisation for Economic Co-operation and Development
OLVC	Organic Law on Villagers' Committees
OS	Other Services
PDC	Pre Degree Course
PHC	Public Health Centre
PMB	People's Militia Battalion
PRC	People's Republic of China
RMB	Renminbi
ROC	Republic of China
SAR	Special Administrative Region
SC	Scheduled Caste
SCP	Special Component Programme
SME	Small and Medium Enterprise
SSI	Small Scale Industry
SSLC	Secondary School Leaving Certificate
ST	Scheduled Tribe
SU	Soviet Union
TC	Trade and Commerce
TSC	Transport, Storage and Communication
TSP	Tribal Sub Plan
UN	United Nations
USA	United States of America
VA	Villagers' Assembly
VC	Villagers' Committee
VEO	Village Extension Officer
VG	Villagers' Groups
VGA	Villager's Groups Assembly
VRA	Villager's Representative Assembly

I

Introduction

Decentralization, democratization, people's participation and sustainable development are serious themes for academic deliberations in India and eighty other countries in the world as world has witnessed unprecedented efforts to decentralize powers from upper echelon to lower level institutions of governance of community level in the past two decades. It is to be noted here that in the same period yet another movement emerged in the world in the name of "Globalization of Economy". Globalization of economy and decentralization of powers are the biggest movements in the world with potentials and threats drawing the attention of the majority of the humanity as they affected the human society. It is a moot question whether globalisation is contradictory or complementary to decentralization. One set of scholars argue that when economy is globalised how can one expect that power will be decentralized. Economy and power will go hand in hand. There is yet another argument projected by another set of scholars that decentralization will help globalization of economy. Through decentralization of powers economic players can get relief substantially from the *raj* of the officials. When more number of power centres are created, companies can deal with the appropriate power centre at their level. It is easy for them to deal with local bodies. There is yet another argument projected that people are given power at the local level to handle new economic dispensation—Globalization of economy, for their own advantage. People will respond both positively and negatively the new dispensation on seeing the implication of new economy at the grassroots. But the discourse on decentralization of powers gained momentum in India after the enactment of the 73rd Amendment to the Constitution of India. The objectives of decentralization of powers vary from country to country. But broader objectives are the same all over the world[1]. As socio-economic problems are on the increase, the gap between the rich and the poor is so vast, frustration of the poor over the performance of the governing institutions is also on the increase, decentralization of powers are considered as one of the solutions to ease out the tension and frustration among the people by accommodating the poor in the process of governance. As a result representative institutions have been broadened.

Before the enactment of the 73rd Amendment to the Constitution of India there were only around 7,000 representatives in India both in National Parliament and State Legislatures. After the enactment of the amendment the strength of the representatives has been increased from 7,000 to 30,07000. Nowhere in the world one can witness this number of representatives. At every level democratic institution is functioning and people's representatives are in a position to look after the felt needs of the people and find solution to the people's problems. Large number of people will be involved in consultative process and in a sense more number of people will be involved in the process of governance. When more number of representatives is recruited, they are to be oriented and sensitized on the roles and responsibilities to be performed by them. One cannot expect a radical change in governance because of the increased number of representatives. Governance is a specialized task and for which elected representatives have to be trained, oriented and capacitated. Moreover, the institutions have to be adequately equipped to make use of the services of the elected representatives. The institutions should have adequate functions, functionaries and finance. It is to be noted here that institutional delivery depends on the environmental settings in which institutions are functioning. There is a marked difference between the functioning of local bodies in industrialized countries and developing countries[2]. It is a well established theory that there is a close correlation between the level of maturity of the citizens and the conditions in which people lead their life will determine the quality of democracy and the effectiveness of service delivery[3].

Many of the developing countries are facing mass illiteracy, mass deprivation, insanitation, inadequate water supply and because of the above problems majority of the people in all those countries are not in a position to lead a decent dignified human life[4]. People have to struggle to get basic minimum facilities to lead their life. When majority are not able to manage their own life how they will contribute for enhancement of democracy and functioning of the governing institutions at the grassroot level is the basic question raised by many in the discourse on local democracy. Further intensive social conflict which is antithetical to democracy has contributed for the poor functioning of the democratic institutions in the developing countries[5]. In India democratic governance institutions have been created through a lengthy Constitution and after fifty years of our experience in democratization and development it has been noticed that the transformative process is not so fast and the governance institutions have helped only the people belonging to the middle class and above. The poor lead life only on hope as Constitution and governments only give promises to the people. The representative institutions could not address the basic issues of the people. It has been realized the existing governance institutions at the federal and state levels do not have the capacity to address the issues of the people. Hence, local governance was thought of[6].

In Indian context the institutions created for governance in the rural areas have to address the issues of poverty, social development of the communities and social justice. But all these issues have to be addressed with the active participation of the stakeholders. The socio-economic development of the people could be achieved through a perspective plan evolved from the community with the meaningful participation of the stakeholders[7]. Apart from the above the local governance institutions have to work for deepening of democracy. Democratization of the society is one of the basic objectives of decentralization of powers. The grassroots institutions particularly the Gram Panchayat is both a representative and a participatory institution. Because of the creation of Gram Sabha in the scheme of Panchayati Raj system the very character of Indian democracy has been changed from representative democracy to participatory democracy. Participation is a process and hence a meaningful design has to be prepared to make or enable stakeholders to participate in the process of governance and development. It is not so easy to make the poor to participate in the process of governance. Equally it is difficult to make the women and the marginalized to participate in governance and development activities. Unless they are empowered, it is highly difficult to make them to be part of the process[8].

Here it is to be recognized that both the Centre and the State governments have openly admitted that they could not achieve economic development and social development for all the disadvantaged segments and hence decentralization is considered as the solution and it is to be implemented. There is a theoretical argument that when a resource rich federal government is not able to address the critical issues of development how can a weak institutional structure with inadequate resource base like the local institutions will address the above issues? It is true that local institutions are weak, structurally, financially and professionally. But they are to address the issues. That is why structure, staff, resources, powers are mandated constitutionally. It needs an array of steps at the local level to equip the institution structurally and financially. The whole process of decentralization has to be seen from the perspective of the regional government's design of the institution, and its operational framework. Because in India, local governance has to be looked after by the State government as per the design of the Constitution. Regional governments are arguing that decentralization of powers devolution from the State government to local governments. Logically speaking there is no scope for committed power devolution from the State governments to local government. Every State government will design local rural governance through conformity legislation according to its own perspective. The institutional design will clearly indicate the focus, perspectives of the State government whether it wants really a well equipped institutional structure to address the critical issues or it wants only an institutional mechanism to show that it conforms the constitutional provisions. At the same time how stakeholders perceive and participate in the governance process at the grassroot matters much. Therefore, the intention and design of the State government and the stakeholder's perception, awareness and commitment to participate in governance at grassroots will decide the course of decentralization of powers[9].

For a meaningful analysis one has to consider the above aspects. On the one hand, the institutional structure, powers and capacity have to be analyzed; and on the other, the stakeholder's perception, perspectives and capacity have to be evaluated. For any evaluation of decentralization of powers there are certain key elements which have to be considered as basic or essential factors. They are: context in which decentralization is conceptualized, "legal framework", strength and capacity of the institutions; capacity of the elected representatives, and the level of awareness of the stakeholders who are getting benefits out of decentralization. Over a period of time approaches have been developed to look at local governance. They are anthropological, sociological, legal, political, administrative, constitutional, economic, and so on. In the same way perspectives have been evolved. The leaders perspectives contributed immensely for shaping of the local governance institutions. The perspective of the leaders on local governance had been developed which is based on their vision on new social and economic order in the society. The leaders perspectives vary from one another on visualising the relationship among three institutions namely state, local governance institutions, and community organizations. The perspective of the leaders are evolved based on their objectives, social reality and the methodology through which they want to achieve the goal of new social order. M.K. Gandhi, B.R. Ambedkar, Jayaprakash Narayan, Jawaharlal Nehru, Rajiv

Gandhi have contributed richly. It needs a thorough analysis in the backdrop of the new dispensation.

But the impact of decentralization of powers has to be seen in terms of democratic values and practices which have been generated and disseminated in the process of governance by involving the people at the grassroots and the services rendered to the public and more particularly the poor and marginalized segments of the society by the grassroots institutions[10]. Since decentralization of powers took place in context where globalization of economy plays its major role analysing of local body institutions which has to be seen in the backdrop of the framework developed by the World Bank and other promoters of the economic globalization[11]. While evaluation the impact of decentralization, it is equally important to look at the impact of globalisation of economy at the grassroots.[12]

In India, the community at the grassroots is hierarchical, feudal, mostly unskilled relying on agriculture for their livelihood, poor in awareness on the process of development, governance and administration. Equally the institutional set-up at the community level is weak in terms of professionalism and facilities. Further, the institutional structure for governance in India was designed by the colonial masters who will rely on the officials rather than the people and it is mere rule and process oriented. Hence, governance and administration are complicated and they cannot be understood easily by the common citizens. The given backdrop will bring a theoretical argument that the existing social and economic environment will not contribute for either promotion of democracy at the grassroot or delivery of services effectively. But the broader assumption is since the decentralization is state driven through a constitutional mandate; claim ability of the entitlements and rights by the stakeholders is high provided there is a mass movement from below[13]. There is yet another argument that while power is devolved to the grassroot institutions with a provision to enable the marginalized to enter into the portals of power, the dominant groups will evolve a design and by which the elites will keep and capture the power[14]. Enough evidences suggest that the struggle is on to capture power by the marginalized and it will take time to fully get the power transferred from the dominant to the oppressed[15].

Near about twenty years have gone after the enactment of the 73rd Amendment to the Constitution for the establishment of a rural local government constitutionally. Despite the initiatives and drives to push decentralization have been done by various agencies in India, one will find a mixture of perception about the progress of decentralization[16]. In India, Kerala has been cited as a progressive State in terms of effective decentralization. It is always argued that States which have got political will demonstrate their commitment through the activities of strengthening of the governance institutions at the grassroots level. Political will on the part of the State government is *sine qua non* for effective decentralization. Decentralization happened even before the 73rd Amendment in West Bengal. In the same way Karnataka also played a crucial role in establishing local governance because of the strong political will of the leaders in Karnataka and West Bengal. But in the post-73rd Amendment era Kerala took a lead as political will had been exhibited and people had been mobilized extensively for decentralization. The high literacy and other human development indicators have enabled the State to move forward in decentralization.

China is yet another country that has embarked in the

process of decentralization of powers. One can visualize from the perspective of the state how China decentralized powers to the grassroot institutions. There is no constitutional mandate for creation of local governance institutions as in India. Yet it takes place vibrantly[17]. How it takes place in China is a curiosity which prompted me to undertake a study in one village unit in China and the same has to be compared with a study on one Gram Panchayat in Kerala. To understand the ground reality, one Gram Panchayat had been taken for analysis. Very interestingly a study was undertaken in China in the lowest unit of governance as Gram Panchayat in India. One unit of the local bodies system was taken for analysis in China. On the same way Gram Panchayat from Indian State Kerala has been selected for analysis. Thus, two units have been covered. But the two units, i.e., one in India and another one in China, have been compared in this study through an ethnographic analysis. But to conduct this study a framework has been evolved. The framework has the following aspects: General overview of the society and politics of the country, brief historical background, local governance framework, structure of the governance at the lowest unit, general administration, transformative process, new administrative structure, governance process, roles and responsibilities, governance structure at village level, strength and weakness, local governance in action, village history basic facts about the village, village economy, facilities available at the village level, women representation, electoral process, state and party politics in village governance and administration, democratic process, innovative activities, culture and livelihood, religious and family functions, conflict and issues.

Though it is a general framework the scholar who has conducted study in China has been asked to cover extensively the village governance, administration, development, and infrastructure, and democracy, cultural and religious life. But the scholar who has conducted study in Kerala has been asked to focus only the basic elements of the local governance and development initiatives of the Village Panchayat leaving other aspects as Indians are aware of many of the aspects of the Indian society, politics and culture. The prime objective of the present work is to show how state regulated society is relying on people and their institutions compared to a democratic state which affirms through Constitution for the creation of rural local governance institution. What are the basic amenities and facilities available in the villages for the benefit of the people in both countries and how these facilities and services are managed by the local institutions in the two countries are brought to light in this work. Apart from the above how democratic process takes place in the villages of both countries as both give different definitions to the same concept democracy. It is an ethnographic study conducted in two villages in India and China. It is not a study about the whole system of Local Bodies. It compares only the village governance settings of China with India through a single case analysis of a village in India and China.

REFERENCES

1. James Manor, *The Political Economy of Democratic Decentralization*, Washington D.C: The World Bank, 1999, pp. 4-11.
2. Anwar Shah (ed), *Local Governance in Developing Countries*, Washington D.C: The World Bank, 2006; Anwar Shah (ed), *Local Governance in Industrial Countries*, Washington D.C: The World Bank, 2006.

3. J.S. Mill, *Utilitarianism: On Liberty and Considerations on Representative Government*, London: Fontana, 1976, pp. 193-195.
4. Pranab Bardhan and Dilib Mookherjee (eds), *Decentralization and Local Governance in Developing Countries: A Comparative Perspective*, New Delhi: Oxford University Press, 2007.
5. Myron Weiner, *The Indian Paradox*, New Delhi: Sage Publications, New Delhi.
6. G. Palanithurai, *Rajiv Gandhi's Vision of Local Governance*, Concept Publishing Company, New Delhi.
7. Rajiv Gandhi Foundation, *The Charter of Panchayats*, Rajiv Gandhi Foundation, New Delhi, 1998.
8. Deepa Narayan (ed), *Empowerment and Poverty Reduction*, Washington D.C: The World Bank, 2002.
9. Satyajit Singh and Pradeep K. Sharma (eds), *Decentralization: Institutions and Politics in Rural India*, Oxford University Press, New Delhi, 2007.
10. Nivaja Gopal Jayal, Amit Prakash and Pradeep K. Sharma (eds), *Local Governance in India: Decentralization and Beyond*, Oxford University Press, New Delhi, 2006.
11. Anwar Shah (ed), *Local Budgeting*, Washington D.C: The World Bank, 2007.
12. G. Palanithurai and R. Ramesh, *Globalisation and Rural Development*, Concept Publishing Company Pvt. Ltd., New Delhi, 2011.
13. G. Palanithurai, "Potentials for Social and Economic Transformation through Decentralized Governance" in D. Sundar Ram (ed), *Panchayati Raj and Empowering People: A New Agenda for Rural India*, Kanishka Publishers and Distributors, New Delhi, 2007.
14. D. Bandyopadhyay "Panchayats and Democracy: Elites *Versus* Dalits" in D. Bandyopadhyay and Amitava Mukherjee (eds), *New Issues in Panchayati Raj*, Concept Publishing Company Pvt. Ltd., New Delhi, 2004, pp146-166.

15. S.N. Chandhary, *Dalit and Tribal Leadership in Panchayats*, Concept Publishing Company Pvt. Ltd., New Delhi, 2004.
16. Institute of Rural Management, *Anand, State of Panchayats Reports 2008-2009: An Independent Assessment*, Ministry of Panchayati Raj, Government of India, New Delhi, 2010, Vols. I and II.
17. Manoranjan Mohanty, Richard Baun, Rongma and George Mathew (ed), *Grassroots Democracy in India and China: The Right to Participate*, Sage Publications, New Delhi, 2007.

II

Rural Local Governance in China

The People's Republic of China: An Overview

The People's Republic of China (PRC – China) is a country in East Asia and its administrative centre and capital city is Beijing. According to the latest 2010 Census, China's population exceeds 1.44 billion people and is ahead India with over 1.21 billion people (Census 2011) the most populous country in the world. It has an approximate territorial size of 9.6 million square kilometres – if including Macao, Hong Kong[1] and disputed (with India) areas such as Aksai Chin, Northern Arunachal Pradesh – which is claimed by China as Southern Tibet – as well as Taiwan[2] as Beijing's claimed 23rd province. Accordingly, the PRC is the third largest country in the world after Russia and Canada and before the USA. Its territory lies within the regional geographical conjunctures of Northeast, Central, Southeast and South Asia with their varying climatic and geological characteristics. Alphabetically listed, China has borders with Afghanistan, Bhutan, India, Kazakhstan, Kyrgyzstan, Laos, Mongolia (largest border), Myanmar, Nepal, North Korea, Pakistan, Russia, Tajikistan and Vietnam.

Politically, the PRC is a single-party socialist republic with the constitutionally anchored leadership of the Chinese Communist Party (CCP). Concerning its administration, the country is divided into 22 (23) provinces, five autonomous regions, four municipalities and two special administrative regions (SAR), namely Hong Kong and Macao. In terms of territorial size Heilongjiang, Inner Mongolia, Sichuan, Qinghai, Xinjiang and Xizang (Tibet) are the largest administrative divisions in the country. Although being home to 56 officially recognized and several more – not officially recognized – minor ethnicities, China's ethnical composition is – in comparison to India – much more homogeneous: more than 91 per cent of the population are ethnic Han and lingua franca throughout the country is Mandarin-Chinese (in China denominated *putonghua*, translated as 'standard language'), a language whose linguistic standards are based on the Beijing dialect. Apart from the People's Republic, it is also official administrative language in Taiwan, where it is known as *guoyu* (national language), and – co-officially with English, Malay and Tamil – in Singapore. It is also one of the official six languages of the United Nations (UN).

Nowadays, provinces and regions where other regional languages are widespread, they are entitled to publicly use them along with Mandarin, while during the early decades of the PRC the use of other languages than Mandarin was discouraged. In this regard – having recognized the necessity of preserving its multi-linguistic and multicultural heritage – China does in the twenty-first century not only grant much more greater freedom of language use in public communication for the many different ethnicities, but also has by enforcement at the same time established a domestic cultural language and lingua franca that is spoken and used throughout the territory and understood by most Chinese citizens and is moreover not easily apprehensible and thus accessible to foreigners.

FIG. 2.1: Provinces of China

Original source: http://www.fas.harvard.edu/~hcf/photos/China_administrative.jpg (Adaption)

Historical Background of China

Summarizing Chinese history in only few sentences is in view of its extent and significance and contribution to world history not only an ungrateful, but also unfair task. Since dealing with the contemporary issue of local governance in China and its comparison to the case of India, the historical part here merely serves as a very short overview. China, although throughout history varying in territorial extension and size, has had a long and quite continuous imperial history of 2,132 years with many different dynasties and yet even pre-Imperial China, of which the contours are still elaborated by archaeologists and historians, adds at least 2,000 years more to the country's civilization-history. Founded by the First Emperor of Qin (*Qin Shi Huangdi*) after the unification of China in 221 B.C., Imperial China lasted until the collapse of the Qing Dynasty in 1911. The subsequent establishment of the Republic of China (ROC) after the collapse of the Qing was followed by a period of about 17 years of territorial separation due to warlordism. Torn by internal conflicts between the authoritarian Nationalist Party (*guomindang* – GMD) and the Communists as well as heavily impacted by the Japanese aggression in 1937 that set off the East Asian scenery of World War II, China again experienced comparably more stability only with the proclamation of the PRC on 1st October, 1949 and the subsequent defeat of the Nationalists and the exile of the ROC to Taiwan. Till today, the small island, which had been occupied by the Japanese for about 50 years, remains a major issue of international dispute and reason of subsequent involvement by the USA as Taiwan's protective power in East Asian affairs, not least in order to check China's economic and political rise.

China's Relations with India

The political relations with India are difficult. Although having shared a common borderline for centuries and despite the experience of strong cultural exchanges, particularly visible in the spread of Buddhism from India to China, regular diplomatic contact was obviated by the geographical constraints of the Himalaya, which largely constrained India's connection to the silk route that connected China with Europe *via* Persia. Political and cultural contacts were rather regular between South India and China, especially between the tenth century Chola kings Rajaraja Chola I and Rajendra Chola and the Song Dynasty emperors. Political and economic contacts became much more intense and stronger in the twentieth century with the Japanese aggression over Asia. After the founding of the PRC, India was one of the early countries to recognize the Communist regime in Beijing (1st April, 1950) and has ever since diplomatically derecognized the ROC on Taiwan.

During the 1950s, India was along with the Soviet Union a major supporter of the PRC's admission to the United Nations Security Council (UNSC), with the China-seat having been occupied by the ROC until 1971. *Hindi-Chini bhai bhai* (Indians and Chinese are brothers) was the motto of Nehru's early foreign policy towards the PRC and New Delhi an important cooperation partner for Beijing, particularly as a communication channel of the Chinese with the UN. Yet, these close relations in the early and mid-1950s converted to a conflicted relationship starting from the late 1950s, when border disputes between the two Asian giants increased. The disputes convoluted in a short, yet tragic war in autumn 1962 that ended with the defeat of a humiliated India and heavy criticism on Nehru's somehow too lax policy on China. Since then, as a consequence of the Cold War era, the two countries have remained suspicious about each other. Since the 1960s, India's leaning towards the Soviet Union — which since early years of close cooperation became one of the greatest fears and concerns of the government in Beijing — has fired Chinese prejudices against India's foreign policy, while India has been sensing a latent hegemonic Chinese foreign policy and is in this regard very concerned about the close Sino-Pakistani relationship. In recent years, conflicting energy policies in South-East Asia, particularly Myanmar, Central Asia, Africa and the Near East as well as India's improved ties with the USA that lead to the heavily disputed Nuclear Deal in 2005 are further bones of suspicions that disturb Sino-Indian relations. These suspicions, having endured into the twenty-first century have, however, not stopped the two countries from fostering good economic relations.

Background of the Province : Jiangsu

Jiangsu Province lies in East China at the East China Sea and borders *inter alia* the prosperous commercial and international metropolis Shanghai. It derives its name from the two most important cities of the province Jiangning (now: Nanjing) and Suzhou and is one of the economically strongest provinces in the country. The total area of the province is 102,600 sq. km with more than 75 million inhabitants with over 45 per cent of them living in rural areas. Jiangsu comprises economically, politically and historically important cities such as Suzhou, Zhenjiang, Changzhou, Yangzhou, Xuzhou, Lianyungang, Kunshan and the province capital city Nanjing, which constitutionally still is the capital city of the exiled ROC.[3] In total, Jiangsu incorporates 1,018 townships and 16,601 administrative villages.

Nanjing served in total six times as capital city for a range of Chinese dynasties and kingdoms, such as the Kingdom of

Wu (11th — 5th century BC) during the Age of the Three Kingdoms (*sanguo shidai*) or during the Tang Dynasty (618 - 907) up to the remains of the ROC nowadays. During the Song Dynasty, Jiangsu experienced an upsurge and has since become a synonym for luxury, wealth and economic development in China.

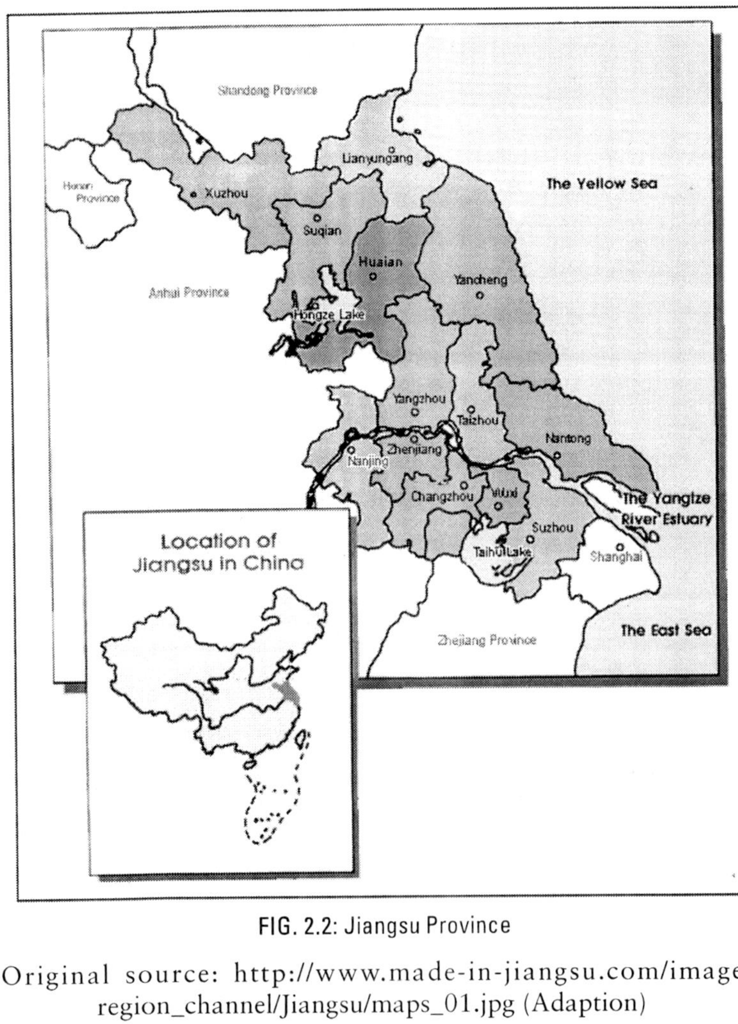

FIG. 2.2: Jiangsu Province

Original source: http://www.made-in-jiangsu.com/images/region_channel/Jiangsu/maps_01.jpg (Adaption)

Local Governance Framework in China

In the course of China's history, local governance underwent fundamental structural and organizational changes that started particularly in the transition period from an imperial monarchy to a republic. After the establishment of the People's Republic of China on 1st October, 1949, the state apparatus began to penetrate the villages in unprecedented detail and alternated not only the established millennia-long structures and organizations, but also minimized the traditionally strong influence of lineages over village governance. This chapter will provide a historical overview about village governance in Chinese history and outline the fundamental administrative changes that took place in over 60 years of the PRC. Following the historical part, the current administrative hierarchy of China, the constitutional position of village governance and an analysis of the *de jure* weaknesses and features of the current system will be explored.

Structure and Governance of Villages in Imperial China

After the successful war campaigns against its six major rival states – Chu, Han, Qi, Yan, Wei and Zhao – thus ending the over 250 years of the Period of Warring States (*zhanguo shidai*), the state of Qin established in 221 BC the first ruling dynasty of Imperial China, comprising the south and east of today's PRC up to the grasslands of Inner Mongolia. Qin Dynasty's famous ruler Yingzheng, who after the unification of the empire called himself the First Emperor of Qin, began —in an effort to ensure the long-term stability of his empire— to structuralize governance. He was the first recorded Chinese ruler to divide his empire into administrative units and established a two-level system of prefectures (*jun*) and counties (*xian*).[4] Although subsequent dynasties extended administrative division to a three-level system, counties remained since Qin-China the deepest formal administrative level of central government outreach[5] for over 2,000 years until the establishment of the PRC.[6] In retro-perspective, counties and villages have been the most consistent units in Chinese history.[7] The historical origins of villages are closely associated with family lineages in Imperial China. The habitations of family clans at a certain place and their demographic, and accordingly geographic, expansion became after years, decades or even centuries villages. While villages in Southern China have predominantly been characterized as mono-lineage villages, villages in the north mostly were of duo- or multi-lineage nature. In villages with one dominating lineage, the family clans chose among themselves — based on factors such as age, experience, education and reputation — suitable members to manage the affairs of the whole community with a lineage head to govern the village. In villages with multiple lineages, power was shared among the different clans while one clan dominated a mono-lineage village.[8] Apart from managing the affairs of a village community, the governing lineages provided goods and services such as education, work opportunities or conflict solutions to the village community.

Since the formal governmental divisions did barely reach to the village — with only few government magistrates and officials per county responsible for a large community of residents — villages had a certain degree of autonomy. The county administration offices (*yamen*) — considering the enormous size of people they were responsible for — easily lost overview about the ongoing affairs, conflicts and problems at the grassroots level of the state. In order to exercise some degree of influence and control on the village-level, they needed the support of the local gentry, which consisted of retired officials and community elites that in many cases even held a degree from the imperial examinations.[9] In many cases, the local gentry assumed thus leadership of their native village, reported from the village and managed the relevant governmental issues and issues at this level. Thus, they were in this role particularly valuable for the imperial government. The local gentry acted as a channel between a village and the county magistrate and as such the formal government. However, despite assuming this intermediary role, the interests of the government and the local gentry conflicted in many cases. Yet, as governmental outreach was limited to county-level and officials in need of support of the local gentry, disputes and conflicts could often not be followed up with punishments.

In view and experience of tumults or peasant revolts, the ruling emperors in later dynasties — in particular the Qing Dynasty (1644 — 1912) – made several attempts to extend its formal power beyond the county-level and introduced control systems to be applied in all over the empire. These systems comprised tax collection and adult-registration (*lijia*), neighbourhood surveillance and criminal control (*bao jia*) and ideological indoctrination (*xiangyue*). The features of these control systems were :

1. The tax collection and registration system of Imperial China was called *lijia* and was already set up during Ming Dynasty (1368 — 1644). According to this system, 110 households were summed up in one *li* and the heads of the ten households with the largest

portion of male adults became — in annual rotation — leaders of a *li* (*lizhang*) while the remaining 100 households were subdivided into *jia*, each *jia* comprising ten households. The *lizhang* supported the government in collecting taxes from their respective *li* and registering male adults (*dingce*).[10]

2. In the early Qing period, the *baojia* system was introduced and referred to the organization of local police that oversaw a fixed number of households to be arranged in a *bao*. One *bao* comprised ten *jia*, with each *jia* made up of ten *pai* and ten households arranged into one *pai*. Thus, each local police unit was to control 1,000 households. *Baojia* assumed - after the later abolishment of the *lijia* system under the Qing responsibility for tax collection which led to misuses and malpractices.[11]
3. During the Song (960 – 1279) and Ming Dynasties, the community covenant (*xiangyue*) system referred to local community organization that was to promote and provide for material aid, instruction, welfare and overall social harmony.[12] This was in line with the neo-Confucian concept of *xiangyue* to ensure social welfare and public order and thus in an educational way combine local self-governance with the obligations by a State government inspired by Confucian ideals.[13] While in the Southern Song Dynasty (1127 – 1279) the *xiangyue* system foresaw particular units to protect society against criminals, fires and care for the sick and poor, its focus changed during the age of the Ming towards a local educational institution.[14]

These mechanisms were — despite official decrees — however not everywhere in place and in many cases set up only superficially.[15] Moreover, the empowered executives undermined the systems by collecting higher taxes from the peasants and by misusing their authority against local rivals. Despite interference and disturbance of peasants through increasing taxes, involvement in local affairs and corrupt officials — having resulted in uprisings that weakened state power — Imperial China did until its final days not really manage to extend direct control to the village level.[16]

Reorganizing Administrative Division during the Republican Years

After the fall of the Qing Dynasty and the founding of the Republic of China (*Zhonghua minguo* – ROC) on 1st January, 1912 by Sun Yat-sen, the ruling Nationalist Party (*Guomindang* — GMD) as well as many of the regional warlords — in view of indirect and rather lose outreach of the past dynasties below county-level — tried to centralize governance and to extend their powers to the village level. China was since the collapse of the Qing Dynasty torn apart into different spheres of influence under the control of regional warlords; administration throughout the country was diverse and chaotic with many peasants being exploited by corrupt officials or even the whole government.[17] Only when GMD leader Chiang Kai-shek, after the successful Northern Expedition[18], managed to either subdue or co-opt the different warlords, China became united on 10th October, 1928 when the last remaining warlord, Zhang Xueliang, joined — under pressure — the national council of the newly proclaimed national government in Nanjing.[19] With the country – although fragilely — united under one flag, the GMD government promulgated in 1928 the county organic law (*xian zuzhifa*) in order to formally establish for the first time an administrative division level below county-level. However, due to ongoing warfare against the communists, the government resorted in fact to the existing *baojia* system and created in 1932 the mutual associated *bao* (*lianbao*) to replace *baojia*, thus it was in fact a fusion of several *bao*. In 1939, the *lianbao* was converted into small town-units (*xiangzhen*) that were administered by one head (*xiangzhengzhang*), one vice-head (*fu xiangzhengzhang*) and several officers.[20]

A major incentive of the national government to enforce control until village level was the creation of the large townships (*daxiang*) in 1941, comprising 1,000 households and thus centralizing all activities of the village administration. Any activities from farming until tax collection were to be regulated and controlled centrally.[21] In view of the ongoing domestic confrontation against the Communists and the already four year-long war against Japan, the Nanjing government was not in the position to enforce this new administrative mechanism and many villages continued with the old practices. Only where the Japanese grabbed hold and tried to structuralize administrative control in their occupied Chinese territories, the system — applied by them — was more successfully implemented.[22]

The enforcement of *daxiang* weakened the existing power structures in the villages and thus the traditional village lineages as well as the local gentry who primarily controlled village affairs for centuries. Lastly, the Guomindangled government of the ROC lost fundamental support within the exploited peasant populace and consequently the battle against the Communist, forcing the remains of the ROC to retreat to Taiwan. [23]

Socialist Penetration of Rural China : The Village in the PRC

Already during the Chinese Civil War against the GMD regime, the Communist Party of China (*Zhongguo gongchandang*) initiated land reforms in 1946 that increased the party's popularity among millions of poor peasants. The land reforms aimed at the expropriation of rich landlords and the distribution of the confiscated land to the poorer peasants.[24] In doing so, the CCP did not only gain much support from the Chinese populace against the unpopular and corrupt GMD regime, but also reduced the power of the traditional rural gentry and family lineages that were considered dangerous opposition against the party rule. The new regime broke the traditional independent family farms that were for centuries the primary institutions of rural China.[25] In July 1949, the CCP started to fully abolish the *baojia* system and established the administrative village (*xingzheng cun*) as the fundamental grassroots level unit of administrative division.[26] Moreover, the state apparatus installed party branches in each administrative village headed by a Party Secretary. Thus, the CCP regime was the first in Chinese history ever to institutionalize regime power even in the smallest administrative level. The administrative villages were staffed with rural cadres and mostly incorporated several natural villages (*ziran cun*). The power of the Party Secretary, who primarily served the interest of the party than the interests of the village, as the highest authority in the administrative village thus further destroyed the existent boundaries and spheres of influences between the different villages and their leading family lineages and rural gentries that had been for centuries a linkage between local societies and the state.[27] With the founding of the People's Republic of China on 1st October, 1949 under the rule of Mao Zedong, the CCP — having experienced the strong power of the peasantry that helped to oust the GMD regime — aimed at consolidating its power by penetrating the villages, since more than 89 per cent of the whole population in that time lived in rural areas.[28]

After the land reforms, the CCP focused its attention on the second step of socialist revolution that was agricultural cooptivization. Rooted in the system of the 1949 introduced Mutual-Aid Teams (MATs)[29], the new regime took on to the collectivization of the millions of rural households. In 1952, about 40 per cent of all peasant households were integrated into MATs, while the regime concurrently continued its socialist experiments by introducing the Agricultural Producers' Cooperatives (APCs).[30] The collectivization experiments proved successful and annual grain output between 1952 and 1958 grew impressively by 22 per cent from 163.9 to 200 million tonnes while the total population grew only by 14.8 per cent, thus providing for an improved average grain supply per citizen.[31] This success of the programme was partly due to gradual — and as compared to the Soviet Union (SU) less radical — approach by the CCP as well as the party's institutional penetration of rural China, having installed branches of the CCP in 90 per cent of all townships (*xiang*) by the end of 1955.[32] This permitted for organizational and ideological guidance of the collectivization programmes in the countryside.

Triggered by this success, CCP leader Mao pushed for spurred industrialization of the country and initiated the Great Leap Forward (*da yuejin* – GLF) that foresaw the mobilisation of China's vast workforce away from the primary sector into the secondary sector. In order to mobilize and pool enough manpower for large-scale industrial projects, a new policy was imposed in 1958 that led within three months to the amalgamation of 753,000 collective farms into 24,000 People's Communes (*renmin gongshe*), comprising a total of 120 million households. The average commune consisted of 5,000 households, 10,000 workers and 10,000 acres.[33] Following the merger of villages and households into enforced communities and separation of families, the People's Communes deprived the most of the peasants from private life with an unmatched penetration of the state apparatus into the life of every Chinese individual. In short, having tremendously shifted workforce from the agricultural to the industrial sector, the GLF resulted in a massive decrease of grain output and within three years more than 30 million people starved to death.[34] The devastating famine not only had detrimental effects to the image of CCP in the population, but also led to shifts in the administrative policy. The mass organizations of People's Communes comprising of 5,000 households each proved to be too large and complicated to manage and their large size was along with natural calamities claimed responsible for the failure of the GLF. Thus, in 1962, the communes were not abolished but reduced in size. The peasants were now organized in production teams (*shengchan dui*) of 20 to 30 households each as the smallest collective unit. The next higher levels were the production brigades (*shengchan dadui*) that comprised several production teams, and — as the largest collective units — the communes, whose quantity grew from 24,000 to 75,000.[35] Resource ownership, production management and accounting for income distribution were delegated to the small production teams.

This administrative system, which fulfilled administrative, social and economic functions, was maintained until the late 1970s.[36]

Reforms of Village Administration and Governance in Post-Mao China

After the death of Mao Zedong on 9th September, 1976, the Third Plenum of the Eleventh Central Committee of the CCP under guidance of Mao's rehabilitated successor Deng Xiaoping decided in December 1978 to initiate major economic reforms. Deng set the pathway for a new policy of reform and opening (*gaige kaifang)* that was to consolidate and improve China's economy. Four Modernizations (*sige xiandaihua)* were officially launched with the objective to make the PRC not only a global economic power, but also to evade the threatening collapse of the Chinese economy.[37] They were also targeted at reducing the prosperity gap between China and Taiwan that was likely to jeopardize Beijing's plans for reunification with the island. Agriculture, science and technology, industry and national defence became subject to modernization in the framework of a socialist market economy.

In 1979, the PRC began to abolish the former dirigiste model of collective agricultural cultivation of the People's Communes and initiated decolllectivization, leading to noteworthy increases in agricultural productivity. In the early 1980s, various rural households began — in opposition to the collective farming system — to turn to single household-based agricultural cultivation.[38] Economically, these local initiatives proved to be very successful and agricultural productivity grew enormously[39], spurring *laissez faire* by the state government that did not curb these incentives and saw them as an experiment of agricultural reform. Following this procedure of intertwined top-down and bottom-up reforms, the state government officially institutionalized the household responsibility system (*jiating lianchan chengbao zerenzhi* — HRS) in 1981.[40] Farming land was distributed among households that were allowed to sell overproduces to the markets after having delivered a quota set by the state government. Although private ownership of land was not possible — which has remained unchanged to date — the government now provided periodically limited land usage rights. The loaning periods have since then increased steadily.

The decollectivization and the introduction of the HRS with the subsequent collapse of the communes, production brigades and the production teams had a significant impact on village governance. The households could now retain post-quota earnings and started to focus on increasing wealth within their own families.[41] At the same time, the state cadres that were before administrative part of the state apparatus' commune hierarchy system were stranded in a new environment. They were the decision-making authorities for peasants on agricultural production. They were stronger than before. Apart from erupting conflicts between the peasants and local cadres that tried to press out more money from the villagers, some cadres quit their posts and joined in the new economic opportunities, thus considerably weakening state power in rural China.[42] Some villagers in Guangxi Autonomous Province seized the opportunity of political vacuum in the villages and created the villagers' committees (*cunmin weiyuanhui*, VC). The state government — spearheaded by the then Vice Chairman of the National

People's Congress (NPC) Peng Zhen[43] — recognized the potential of limited grassroots level self-administration and village elections as a way to decrease tensions between the peasants and the local cadres and to instal mutual supervision of villagers and cadres, thus enabling the party to consolidate its power in the rural areas.[44] Again in an interactive procedure of bottom-up initiatives and top-down encouragement and legitimization, the state government integrated the VC into the formal administrative hierarchy of the People's Republic of China in 1982. The communes were abolished and replaced by township governments, the production brigades were replaced by administrative villages.[45] The production teams merged into villagers' groups (*cunmin xiaozu*, VG).

Following debates within the state government about the advantages and dangers of providing a framework for village elections, Peng Zhen pushed the NPC to pass the Organic Law on Villagers' Committees (OLVC) in 1987. On a trial basis, the law defined scope, functions and powers of the Villagers Committees and provided the legal and institutional framework for village elections that should be conducted experimentally-wise. In the aftermath of the crackdown of protests on the Tiananmen Square in 1989, Peng Zhen even managed to beware the OLVC from being sacked and abolished by the state government.[46] According to data from the Ministry of Civil Affairs, half of all Chinese villages in 1994 had conducted elections and 25 provinces adopted a localized version of the OLVC.[47]

The experiments with local elections and their limitations were manifold since the passing of the trial version of the OLVC. Many villages conducted non-competitive elections or semi-competitive elections. In non-competitive elections, the number of candidates equals to the number of positions, while in semi-competitive elections, one or two more candidates than available positions can be elected.

Open nominations were experimentally conducted in the election process of villages in Lishu county, Jilin province and officially promulgated as election standard by the county government in 1993. In this comparably open method called *haixuan* (literal meaning: ocean election), every voter casts a ballot nominating his preferred candidates. Those with the most nominations are eligible for final elections. The ballot-casting process of semi-competitive elections along with the *haixuan*-method of open nominations became the standard requirement for VC elections in the revised OLVC in 1998.[48] Since then, elections have been conducted in all villages throughout China, though their qualities differ from place to place. Yet, regulations on village governance and elections are still in a process of amendment and change. The newest development here is the amendment of the OLVC whose draft was first published for public discussion and comments in 2009[49] and finally implemented on 28th October, 2010.[50]

Village Administration in China — Structural and Legal Aspects

According to Article 30 of the Constitution of the People's Republic of China[51], the Administrative hierarchy of the country consists of three levels. Originally, the highest level below the Central Government (*zhongyang zhengfu*) is the province-level (*shengji xingzhengqu*). Below province-level there are counties (*xianji xingzhengqu*) and below counties the township-level (*xiangji xingzhengqu*).[52] A further level of sub-national state administration — prefecture (*diji xingzhengqu*) — under the province level has been aggregated to the three-level structure and is implemented in every province except for the two Special Administrative Regions (*tebie xingzhengqu*) Hong Kong and Macao as well as the municipalities directly under the Central Government, namely Beijing, Chongqing, Shanghai and Tianjin.[53] There is also a fifth level, village (*cunji xingzhengqu*), which from the constitutional perspective only has limited administrative competences and is merely local[54], but nevertheless plays in reality a significant role in domestic politics.[55]

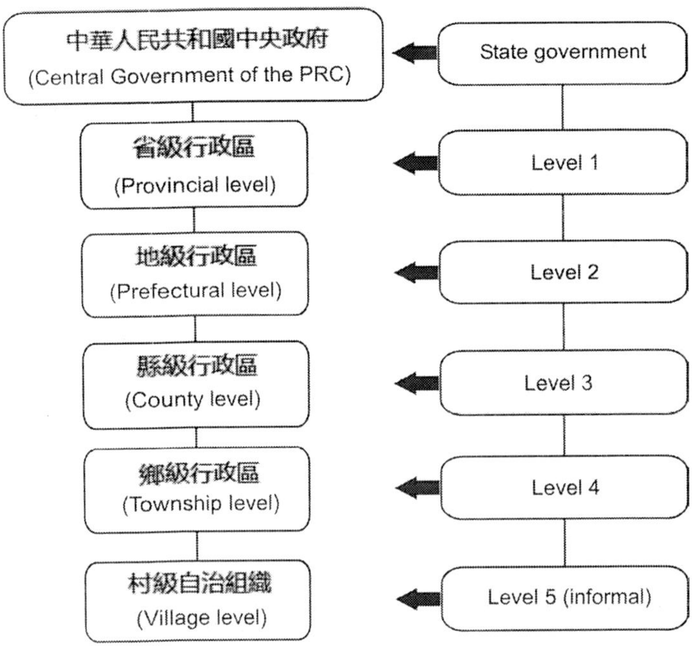

Fig. 2.3: Administrative Hierarchy of the PRC

Village Governance in Contemporary China: Constitutional and Legal Position

The village (*cun*) is the basic-level unit in the administrative hierarchy of the PRC and appears in two categories that are administrative villages and natural villages. Administrative villages usually comprise several natural villages as well as rural neighbourhoods and communities which in China are formal divisions with defined boundaries and heads. As outlined in §111 of the Constitution of the People's Republic of China, an administrative village is administered by a VC that is presided by a village leader (*cunzhang*).[56] Heads of VCs and committee members are elected by popular vote every three years. §111 also stipulates that villagers' committees are to set up sub-committees that shall handle public affairs and goods, mediate in disputes between villagers, help to uphold public order and ensure safety and health of the villagers. VCs are also required to communicate the opinions, demands and suggestions from their respective villagers to the People's Government[57]. The following sections will outline in detail the national constitutional and legal positions of the different bodies involved in the process of village governance as well as describe the national legislation for village-level elections.[58]

Powers and Duties of the Villagers Committee according to the OLVC

§111 of the Constitution of the People's Republic of China as well as §2 of the OLVC define VCs as "self-governing grass-roots level organizations of mass character" (*jiceng qunzhongxing zizhi zuzhi*). A VC consists of minimum three and maximum seven people, namely one head (*zhuren*) — the village leader, one vice head (*fuzhuren*) and at least one to maximum four committee members. §6 of the OLVC additionally stipulates the mandatory requirement of female members in the VC as well as committee members from ethnic minorities for villages that have different ethnic minority groups. As per law the villagers committees shall support the economic and social development of the village, to protect and improve the environment of the village, ensure the equality between men and women as well as the equitable access and use of natural resources by the villagers. They are moreover expected to disseminate the constitution, laws and policies of the national government, including the very unpopular and much criticized national birth control policy (*guojia jihua shengyu zhengce*).[59] In order to carry out these duties, the villagers committee can establish sub-working committees for conflict mediation, public order, health and birth control. Members of the VC may concurrently assume a post in a sub-committee. In villages with few population, however, there is no requirement to install of sub-committees and related work can be share among the committee members.

Further Organs and Institutions of Local Governance as defined by the OLVC

(A) Villagers' Assembly

The Villagers' Assembly (VA) controls, discusses and comments the work of the VC and involves in issues such as land contracting and distribution, usage and distribution of the gains of the village's economy and projects that are in the public interests of the villages. All villagers that meet the age requirement of at least 18 years can join the VA. The VA can formulate and change the regulations of self-governance of the village and report and accord this changes to the next higher-level, the township government. It can be convened upon proposition by the VC, by 10 per cent of all villagers or by one-third of the assembly of the villagers' groups (VGA). The convention must be publicly announced 10 days prior to its session.

(B) Villagers' Representative Assembly

Larger villages can establish a Villager's Representative Assembly (VRA) which can be conceived as a standing committee of the VA.[60] In the case of the case study of province Jiangsu, it determines the total size of the post-election VC. The VRA is constituted by members of the VC and representatives of five to ten households or VG representatives. The latter are selected representatives of a bunch of five to 15 households or a certain number of people selected by the VG — whereas the villagers representatives shall constitute more than four-fifth of the VRA with women making over one-third of the VRA. The VRA is convened by the VC at least once every three months. Likewise, one-fifth of the representatives of the VRA can also convene a meeting.

(C) Villagers' Groups

Villager's Groups (VG) are pooled households of different neighbourhoods of the village. The head of the VG (*cunmin xiaozu zuzhang*) is — like the VG — elected for a term of three years, equalling to the duty term of the VC, and represents his VG in the VRA. In the example of Jiangsu Province, the VGs choose the election committee for the VC elections. Moreover, as a successor of the production teams, the VG is in most parts of China involved in one of the most crucial issues in contemporary Chinese rural politics that is the management, distribution and supervision of land. The

VG can be convened by two-third of all the participants of the different VG that are over 18 or by two-third of all household representatives engaged in the VG.

(D) Village Branch of the CCP

Since the VCs are not part of the formal state bureaucracy, the CCP has in every village local party branches, ensuring the village self-administration does not challenge the leadership of the CCP. In nearly every village there is a local branch of the CCP.

Legally and also in praxis, the powers of the party-organ are always supreme to those of the administrative body. More problematic is, that there is no clear definition and separation of competences between the leaders of the two bodies. Albeit self-governance on the village-level is formally stipulated in the constitution and the OLVC, democratic freedom in the one-party state of the PRC is, however, constrained by the claim for political supremacy of the CCP that the party, not least for reasons of political stability and unity of China, does not want to be challenged. In §4 of the OLVC it is stated, that village-level branch of the CCP has "leading core function and (exercises) guidance and support to the VC in carrying out its duties". Thus, the party branch of the CCP is an integral part in the village. This does mean nothing else than a substantial involvement, yet even control by the ruling party in the process of village governance to avoid any challenge to the party leadership or village policies that do not comply with national policies. Thus, the village cadres are both agents of the state and the party as well as – being locals – normally strongly attached to the interests of their villages.

The substantial involvement of the state apparatus and thus of the CCP's national policies in village governance can particularly be seen in §9 and §30 of the OLVC, where the VC is required to promote, publicly promulgate, carry out and supervise the very unpopular national birth control policy that has been a heavy burden to the traditional ample family lineage structures, being significantly reduced in size. Another mirror of the limitations of self-governance are outlined in §3, where the establishment, dissolution and scope of the VC is put forward by the township government, which – after the consent of the VC – can then be approved by the county government. Although the township governments are not allowed to meddle in the affairs of the village, the stipulation of §3 enables the township government to exercise a check-and-block-policy, compromising the democratic value of village-elections. Moreover, §34 requires the VC to establish archives where casted ballots in elections, meeting protocols, land distribution contracts and other accounting data are diligently registered. This, in theory, does not only provide the state with substantial supervision of the ongoing activities in the village as well as the ballot casting of the voters, but also opens the door for related governmental involvement in the private affairs of the villagers and eventual political and legal sanctions for those who are regarded as a threat to the state apparatus.

On the other hand, the amended OLVC stipulates the regular publication of information on issues such as land contracts, financial accounting and collective property management by the VC, thus ensuring greater administrative transparency within the village. In addition to this, the VC is required to establish a village service control committee (*cunwu jiandu weiyuanhui*) as supervising body.

Local Governance in Action — China — Mengzibang Village

Introduction

Village governance and elections in China are not unitary, but rather manifold. There varying degrees of autonomy, fairness, democratic freedom or representation of minorities and women between each of the 31 province-level units. In this regard, this case study can only be exemplary. In view of the comparison with Akathethara Grama Panchayat in the much advanced Indian State of Kerala, Jiangsu Province as a prosperous and rich province for the Chinese part of the local governance case study was chosen. Apart from economics, the choice of studying a village in Jiangsu is also geared to the higher degree of democratic freedom to determine governance as compared to other province-level units. For the case study, the small village Mengzibang was randomly selected.

After a brief historical background, the characteristics of the village will be introduced. After that, the chapter proceeds to analyse village self-administration in Mengzibang, providing a comprehensive overview on its performance in the Chinese context.

Historical Background of Mengzibang

Mengzibang has a long history that dates back more than 1,000 years. Being located in immediate proximity to Jinxi Township, the village has witnessed a major historical event during the reign of the Song Dynasty which will be presented here in brief. The Song, which from 960 to 1127 ruled over most of inner, northern and southern China – and therefore denominated as Northern Song Dynasty[61] — were since 1125 at war with their former ally, the Jurchen (also known as Jin Dynasty) which increasingly pressed southwards from northern China. After the Jurchen seized the Song capital Kaifeng in 1127, the imperial court moved to Lin'an (today's Hangzhou) and sought to regain control over its lost northern territories. Crown prince Zhao Wei, Song Emperor Gaozong's[62] only successor, decided to accompany his father to combat the approaching Jurchen troops. Not far from Lin'an, the Jurchen had already occupied Yangzhou. Zhao Wei's two capable mistresses concubine Chen (*Chen fei*) and concubine Ge (*Ge fei*), who had a deep understanding of martial arts and military strategies, asked the crown prince to let them go with him. Zhao Wei agreed and the troops marched towards Lin'an.

Photograph 2.1: Panoramic View of Mengzibang

Photograph 2.2: Water Burial Sites of the Concubines Chen and Ge

Then they arrived at the battle side, Gaozong and Zhao Wei learnt about a mutiny among the Jurchen troops which resulted in the assassination of their commander Emperor Hailingwang and the retreat of the troops to Yanjing (former name of Beijing). In order to ensure that this was not a trick, Gaozong asked Zhao Wei to stay in Lin'an for a while. On the occasion of their success against the Jurchen, Zhao Wei celebrated this in a big banquet. Unfortunately, concubine Chen fell ill during the banquet and, since Zhao Wei and his troops could not find a medic in time, she died three days after having suffered from three days of heavy stomach aching. Following her death, the emperor commissioned a geomancer to find a burial site. Jinxi town was identified to be the final place of concubine Chen's tomb. There her coffin was, after a large ceremony, escorted by Zhao Wei to the water burial site. Not much later, concubine Ge also died of illness was according to her wish also buried along with Chen in Jinxi. Therefore, Jinxi and its surroundings are nowadays particularly referred to as the burial sites of these two imperial concubines, making it a popular destination for Chinese tourists.

Basic Facts about the Village

Mengzibang is a small administrative village in rural south-eastern Jiangsu Province. East of Jiangsu's Great Lake (*Dahu*), it lies within a flatland area pervaded by small rivers and encircled by two small lakes, the Yangmintian lake and the Bailian (white lotus) lake. Mengzibang is part of and lies few kilometres north-east to Jinxi township, the latter belonging to the county-level city Kunshan which lies within the prefecture-level city of Suzhou. Mengzibang borders Zhangpu town and is an administrative merger of two formerly separate natural villages, namely Mengzibang and Gemu which are connected *via* the Kunjin road and water channels. The population of the village is growing slowly but steadily. A total of 2,989 long-term residents live in Mengzibang. Out of these about 1,200 reside in the part of Gemu village and about 1800 live in the part of Mengzibang village, with a total of 877 registered peasant households. The village society of Mengzibang is quite homogeneous. Nearly every villager belongs to the Han ethnicity. The village has a total area of over 3,800 mu[63]. The cultivated land of the village covers an area of around 3,762 mu, of which 2,188 mu are used for producing special plants and 1,574 mu for grains and oils. Fish ponds cover 1,656 mu. The village has had a long agricultural tradition, particularly in terms of growing rice paddy. This tradition is also reflected in the older denomination for Mengzibang. It was formally known under the name Yangtian, which literally means "rice seedling bed".

Photograph 2.3: Satellite View of Mengzibang and Gemu

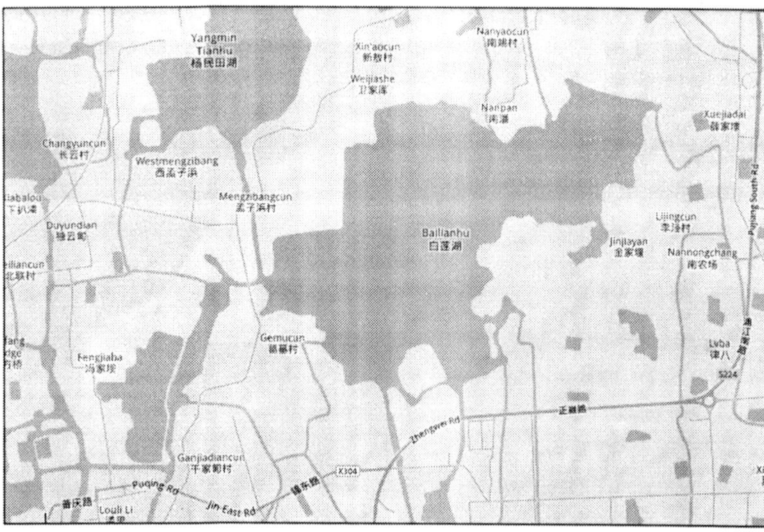

Photograph 2.4: Map of Mengzibang and Gemu among other Villages in the Area

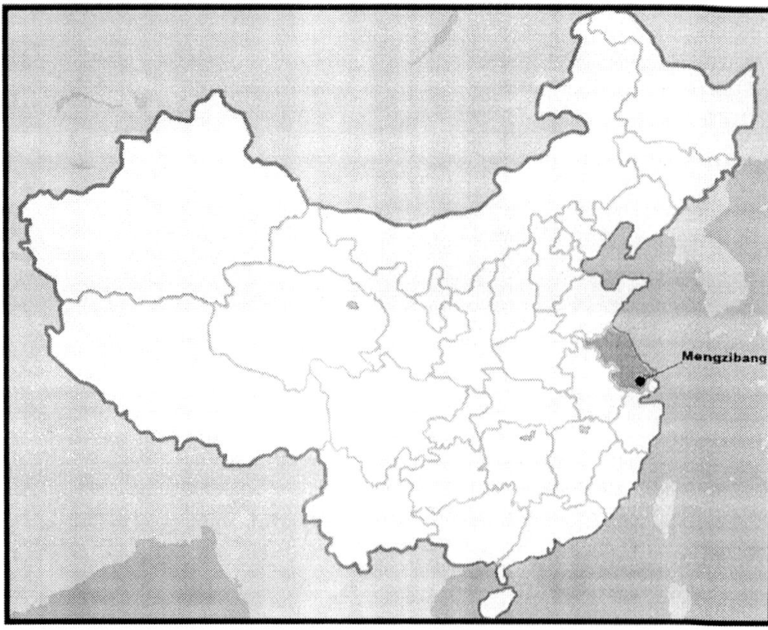

Photograph 2.5: Location of Mengzibang within Jiangsu Province

Table 2.1: Basic Statistics about Mengzibang

Total area	*2.53 sq. km*	*Residents in Mengzibang part*	*ca. 1800*
Cultivated land	2.51 sq. km	Residents in Gemu part	ca. 1200
=> cultivation of special plants	1.45 sq. km	Density whole village	1181 people/sq. km
=> cultivation of grains	1.04 sq. km	Total registered households	877
Fishpond area	1.10 sq. km	Long term residents/household ratio	3.4 people/household
Actual residents	2820 people	Literacy	100%
Long term residents	2989 people		

Source: Computed.

Table 2.2: Economic Division

Agricultural labour	*Industrial labour*	*Service labour*	*Other labour*	*Total*
121	891	494	63	1569

Source: Computed.

Public Facilities and Village Economy

Although not remote, due to its comparably small size there are no hotels, restaurants, post offices, banks, schools or hospitals directly in the village but only on the township level-area in nearby Jinxi. Yet, Mengzibang has a small dispensary health centre. Five years before, the village also had a primary school which was then closed and the former school facilities sold to a manufacturer of electrical appliances. The closest school is located in Jinxi town. The village has also a library with a stock of over 1,000 books, a function hall for a variety of cultural, social and other functions as well as a theatre stage hall. Further public facilities include activity centres for old and disabled people, a multifunctional and a rehearse hall. The various administrative divisions, associations and the local branch CCP are accommodated within the newly constructed public service centre.

For the safety and cleanliness of the 728 metres long Gemu River that flows through the two parts of the village, two contact staff officers from the city river management office are located in the village. Every household, official institution and industrial facility as well as agricultural undertaking in the village has a water supply connection, yet — in view of this — there are nearly no public taps. The water quality is good, yet not as consumable as tap water for example in Central Europe. The village has a local police branch with six police officers – including one lead officer – whose name and contact details for emergency cases are displayed at the local police office.

Table 2.3 : Overview of Public Facilities in Mengzibang

Anti-heresy warning education room (*fan xiejiao jingshi jiaoyu shi*)	Activity room for disabled and ill people (*canbingren huodong shi*)
Board and card games room (*qi pai shi*)	Health centre (*zhenliaosuo*)
Library (*tushuguan*)	Multi-functional hall (*duo gongneng ting*)
Non-native registration service centre (*wailai renkou dengji fuwuzhan*)	Police office (*gong'an bangongshi*)
Public order comprehensive administration office (*shehui zhi'an zonghe zhili bangongshi*)	Public service centre (*gongong fuwu zhongxin*)
Rehearse hall (*payan ting*)	River management contact office (*Kunshanshi Jinxizhen cunji hedao guanli lianxi bangongshi*)

Source: Computed.

Photograph 2.6: Pinboard at the Police Office with Contact Details of the Local Police Officers

Photograph 2.7: Public Offices in Mengzibang

Communication Facilities

Mengzibang is a village that features — apart from normal tarred pathways — water channels that are rarely seen in villages in East China. This water channels have in ancient times been important for intra- and inter-village transport of persons and produces, to wash clothes or for fishery. Manually driven boats have historically been made of a combination of wood and stones and these characteristics are still being preserved in Mengzibang to date.

Mengzibang directly adjoins Jiangsu's X206 County Road, which connects Jinxi and Kunshan, and *via* nearby S26 Huchang Expressway it is also linked to the international metropolis Shanghai in the east and Suzhou in the west. This connection is very important for the village, since due to its small size the village lacks a range of important public facilities.

The pathway and alley (*hutong*) connectivity — which is a traditional characteristic of many Chinese towns and villages — as well as the infrastructure within the village are likewise very good and every habitat is connected by pathways, roads and/or bridges.

Photograph 2.8: One of the Many Water Channels and Transportation Boats in Mengzibang

An interesting and characteristic feature of the village is the many tiger emblems that can be found on the walls of the upper compartments of several buildings in the village. Standing on bridges or in narrow alleys, there are usually Tiger emblems on both ends of the respective alley or bridge. These Tiger emblems, as interviewed villagers pointed out, are protection symbols of these pathways and the village and its inhabitants on a whole against evil and demons.

Photograph 2.9: A Hutong (Alley) in Mengzibang

Photograph 2.10: Tiger Emblem as seen from a Bridge in Mengzibang

Electronic communication facilities in Mengzibang are very advanced and every household is since the late 1980s electrified. Yet, during the 1980s only every 40th household, and particularly the wealthier ones, had electrical appliances like TVs. This situation changed in the early 1990s when TVs, cell phones, washing machines, fridges and computers increasingly became common equipment in the village households. Nowadays, some households have even installed advanced solar heater systems that provide warm water in cold winter days — a technology, which is more widespread in Mengzibang than in a common Central European village. Most of the village households do not use landline telephone connections and rather resort to cell phone communications. Moreover, many households in Mengzibang have internet access, enhancing social exchange— and business possibilities.

Structure of the Village Economy

Jiangsu-Shanghai-Zhejiang (JSZ) belt, Mengzibang is comparably far more developed and richer than many other villages in rural China, especially compared to those in the more western provinces like Qinghai or Gansu. However, within this administrative village there are gaps in development. Mengzibang part is much more developed than Gemu. The economy of the village is in a clearly visible process of transformation from an — increasingly mechanized — agricultural to an industrialized village, which is associated by some villagers with feelings of mounting pressure. The village economy is characterized by three sectors: traditional agriculture and fishery, electronic hardware manufacturing and recycling of waste products.

In total, there are 30 companies in and around the village with a Taiwanese manufacturer of electrical appliances and an export-oriented clothing manufacturer constituting the larger ones. Moreover, there are several small privately owned workshops producing clothes and processing metals like gold, tin and silver in the village as well as other small individual workshops with annual profits ranging from 40,000 to 50,000 RMB. In every larger block area there are also small shops selling food and items for everyday use. Mengzibang has also one clothing shop and a jeweller.

Photograph 2.11: Being located in prosperous and economically strong East China within the reach of the ongoing rural transformation in the people's Republic of China

Photograph 2.12 : Small Shop in Mengzibang

Within the township level-area there are numerous small and medium enterprises (SMEs) and workshops providing jobs for the dwellers from surrounding villages. Thus, apart from running own small commodity shops and companies, the nearby job opportunities in factories or in the farmlands lead to the effect, that the majority of the (male) villagers from Mengzibang work within the township level-area or even in the village itself, with only few working in more distant places on the county-level or higher. The female villagers usually do not work outside the village but in the fields. Many villagers do animal husbandry, mostly raising Chicken and ducks in the courtyards in front of their houses or in small encircled compounds on the street or side of the Gemu river. There are still some villagers that engage in traditional skills like artisan and carpentry. Some households also generate incomes by renting out their apartments. In 2009, the average income per working villager was 14,917 RMB.

The locals are inclined to save lots of their income and only spend a small amount to prepare for larger investments, such as houses or cars. This high level of wealth is for example mirrored by in the car per household rate in Mengzibang: many households in the villages possess a car and there are households who do not only own Chinese but also international brands from Germany and Korea.

Structure of Village Administration and Governance Activities

As an administrative village, Mengzibang features — in line with the requirements stipulated in the Jiangsu Province Election Legislation (JSEL) — all mandatory entities of local

Photograph 2.13: The Banner Reads: "Build a Democratic Village, Construct a Civilized and Harmonic Countryside!" A Harmonic Society is the Major Objective of the Current Chinese Leadership

governance whose legal roles, duties and systemic weaknesses were already introduced in chapter three. The VC of Mengzibang consists in the current tenth legislature period (2011 – 2013) of five people — among them one female member — and includes one head who is the incumbent Village Head and concurrently holds the post of Vice-Party Secretary (*fu shuji*), which is not only exemplary for the substantial power of the CCP in the governance of Mengzibang, but also a democratic confirmation of their legitimacy among the villagers.

While the head of the VC, the village leader, supports and coordinates the overall work of the committee, the other members manage issues such as public security or military management. The only female committee member is responsible for the financial accountancy of the VC. All except for one member of the VC are party members of the CCP, underlining not only the party's leading core function and guidance of the VC in carrying out its duties as stipulated in §4 of the OLVC, but also their acceptance by the villagers who voted for them. The VC of Mengzibang is assigned six subordinate working committees (*cunweihui xiashe gongzuo weiyuanhui zuzhi*) which reflect its main working domains. The working domains comprise: production and construction (*shengchan jianshe*), civil mediation (*renmin tiaojie*), social security (*shehui baozhang*), public safety (*zhi'an baowei*), cultural and educational hygiene (*wenjiao weisheng*) and elderly people's work (*laoling gongzuo*). All these working committees comprise four members including one (committee) leader, except for the latter committee which has in total three members. It is clearly visible that there is a high degree of post castling in the sub-committees between members of VC and members of the CCP.

Table 2.4 : Villagers' Committee of Mengzibang

Name	*Sex*	*VC Position*	*Education*	*Function*	*CCP Member/Position*
Xiao Qiaoquan	Male	VC Head	College	Coordination overall work of the VC	Yes, Vice-Secretary
Xie Meiying	Female	VC Member	Polytechnic	Financial accountancy	Yes, Member
Cao Xuedong	Male	VC Member	College	PMB commander and group secretary	Yes, Member
Zhu Zequan	Male	VC Member	JMS	Team accountancy	Yes, Member
Zhang Xulong	Male	VC Member	JMS	Director public security	No

Table 2.5 : VC Working Committees

Production and construction	*Zhang Xulong* (working committee leader) Zou Jin'an Yuan Aer Zhao Aimei
Civil mediation	Xie Qiaoquan (working committee leader) Xu Fangming Zhu Zequan Cao Xuedong
Social security	Xie Meiying (working committee leader) Zhang Xulong Cao Xuedong Xu Fangming
Public safety	Zhu Zequan (working committee leader) Xu Fangming Cao Xuedong Zhang Xulong
Cultural and educational hygiene	Cao Xuedong (working committee leader) Xie Meiying Zhang Xulong Zhu Zequan
Elderly people's work	Zhao Aimei (working committee leader) Xu Aqiao Cheng Yin'gen

Mengzibang's VRA consists in total of 59 representatives with all members of the VC, CCP branch office and their working groups being members, too. Apart from the VC and

Table 2.6: Villagers' Groups and their Leaders

VG	*VG leader*	*CCP member*	*VG*	*VG leader*	*CCP member*
Group 1-2	Zou Axing	Yes	Group 11-13	Zhu Zhenglin	No
Group 3-4	Tang Ada	Yes	Group 14-16	Cao Xuedong	Yes
Group 5-6	Zou Jin'an	Yes	Group 17-18	Gong Peigen	Yes
Group 7-8	Chen Asan	Yes	Group 19-20	Zhao Taosheng	Yes
Group 9-10	Yuan Aer	Yes			

its sub-committees, there are 20 VGs in Mengzibang — originating from the former production teams. All but one of their heads are party members:

Women Representation

The situation of women in Chinese villages has improved and chauvinism is not that prevalent in rural China as it has been until decades before. Although female village leaders are very rare in China (mostly women serve as deputy leaders) — and that is also true for Mengzibang — their representation in public offices has quantitatively increased. Similar to the regulation of reservations for certain social groups in India, the provincial legislation for elections of Jiangsu province requires representation for women and ethnic minority groups among the final candidates for the VC elections, thus avoiding nomination bias against potentially good female candidates. However, in the end they are also subject to the voters' decision in the election process.

In Mengzibang, women are represented in the village administration mainly by engaging in the domains of general female issues, birth control — a major aspect of state policy in the village administration process — and financial accounting. The latter assignment has also a cultural connotation, since women in Chinese families traditionally are responsible for handling and administering the household finances while men need to bring them in. Yet, as compared to their male counterparts, they still only make a small percentage of those in the village administration.

The Election Process in Mengzibang

Mengzibang is one of the early villages that had introduced grassroots level elections, with the tenth election having taken place at the end of December 2010. The VC of Mengzibang is since the first elections in 1984, an integral part of the administration of ancient village. The elections are financed by each village and only in cases of lacking finances, the higher level county government may help the village. All members of the VC in Mengzibang, including the head and the Vice head need to undergo a formal election process that takes place every three years with possible re-election of each candidate, thus following suit the stipulations of the OLVC and the JSLE. The villagers' representative assembly determines the total size of the post-election VC which must at least consist of three and maximum of seven people. In the case of Mengzibang, the size of the VC for the last election was fixed at five people. For the purpose of elections, an Election Committee (EC), which as stipulated by Article 7 of the JSEL consist of five to nine committee members, has to be set up. The committee members are chosen by the villagers' assembly or the villagers groups. The EC members choose among themselves a head who oversees the work of the EC. The committee members may not run as candidates for the VC.

The formal requirements for casting a ballot are stipulated by §10-12 of the JSLE :

(a) minimum voting age is 18;
(b) voters (and also candidates) must register as such;
(c) villagers with permanent residence registration and living in the village can cast a ballot;
(d) those who are not officially registered resident of the village but live and work they may request permission from the EC; and
(e) Absentee voting is possible upon consent of the EC. Entrusted representatives may have a maximum of three absentee votes.

Article 10 of the JSLE explicitly mentions that both for candidates and voters there may be no restriction in joining the elections due to their race, sex, profession, family, religion, level of education, financial standing or length of residence. The only one exempted from the voting or running as candidates are those people who are deprived from their political rights.

20 days prior to the election, a list of all people who are permitted to cast votes in the following VC election process is published. The lists can be amended upon complaints or changes filed at the EC maximum 10 days prior to the elections. The election committee then decides within seven days about eventual amendments and eventually publish a revised list. Candidates for the VC election are nominated by all registered voters through the *haixuan*-method. The election committee then publishes a list of all candidates for the VC. The JSLE requires that candidates for the VC must be educated, law-abiding, honest, fair and lead the village to prosperity.

A candidate that achieves a quorum of over 50 per cent is elected. If more candidates than VC seats meet less than 50 per cent quorum, then those candidates with more votes win. In case of equal numbers, run-off elections with relative majority are conducted. If less candidates than VC seats meet less than 50 per cent quorum, a second round of election is conducted where the candidate must achieve a relative majority of at least one third of the votes. The EC oversees the ballot and calls out the names of those voted for while counting. The final list of the selected candidates is published after the counting, provided that there were no irregularities in terms of fairness and impartiality have occurred during the election process.

Photograph 2.14: Wall with the Lists of Names All Eligible Voters for the Elections for the Tenth VC

Characteristics and Problems of Local Governance

While the VC is elected, other key offices and positions such as that of the local party secretary are filled upon appointment by the government. Chapter three has already outlined that the self-administrative traces of village governance in rural China are checked by local branch offices of the CCP. They provide for the dissemination and execution of national policy guidelines and ensure that locally elected VC members adhere to these policies. A comparison between the overall Three-Year Plan objectives of Mengzibang's VC for the period between 2008 and 2010 and those of the local CCP branch show a very high correlation and are exemplary for the joint governance of both locally elected and party appointed leaders. The CCP branch office in Mengzibang has five members that cover different working domains regarding the administration of the village: one secretary, who is responsible for the overall organization of the party in this village, two deputy secretaries with one of them assisting the secretary and one supporting the work of the VC, one discipline-inspection commissioner (*jijian weiyuan*) who is responsible for issues of the local village economy (agricultural and industrial production) and one female propaganda commissioner (*xuanchuan weiyuan*), responsible for the handling of all issues and tasks in Mengzibang which are related to finance, social safety and birth planning. They are assisted by several staff workers who cover the issues of technology usage and market economic training, civil mediation, promulgation of national policies, public security or promotion of "culturally civilized behaviour" — all in accordance with national level directives and policies.

Table 2.7: CCP Branch Office of Mengzibang

Name	*Sex*	*Education*	*Position*	*Work assignment*
Zou Xin'gen	Male	College	Secretary	Coordinate overall work of the party branch
Xu Fangming	Male	Polytechnic	Vice Secretary	Assisting work of the Party branch
Xie Qiaoquan	Male	College	Vice Secretary	Taking care of overall work of the VC
Gao Jianfu	Male	JMS	Discipline Inspection Commissioner	Agricultural sidelines production
Xie Meiying	Female	Polytechnic	Propaganda Commissioner	Financial affairs, social safety and birth planning

Photograph 2.15 : Office of the Party Branch in Mengzibang along with Other Local Governance Offices in the Village's Public Service Centre

Table 2.8 : CCP Branch Office Members and their Responsibilities

Name	*Position Title*	*Responsibilities*
Zou Xin'gen	Dual-band modelling	(a) Initiate the cultivation of knowledge on practical technologies and market economy; (b) Promote the advance of practical technologies in the village; (c) Disseminate every kind of technological knowledge of the party to the people; and (d) Instruct, spread and demonstrate technology.
Xie Qiaoquan	Civil mediation	(a) Get closely in touch with the people, understand deeply their situation and help to solve their actual difficulties in time; and (b) Help 1-2 destitute households and support them in solving their life problems.
Xu Fangming	Policy dissemination	(a) Actively develop propaganda and education on legal systems and rural and folk law; (b) Initiatively communicate to the party branch or concerned departments the public order situation; and (c) Assist in handling public order problems according to law.

(Contd).

Table 2.8 (*contd.*)

Name	*Position Title*	*Responsibilities*
Yuan Aer	Villagers support and integration	(a) Immerse into the investigation and study of the people; (b) Handle civil disputes and other various kinds of stability factors; (c) Help the VC to mediate civil disputes and settle contradictions; and (d) Put forward reasonable suggestions to safeguard social stability.
Zhu Zequan	Safeguarding of public order	(a) Initiate the participation and support the party branch in developing healthy and useful cultural and recreational activities in the village; and (b) Actively propose new cultural trends; (c) Get rid of superstition in the village and boycott every kind of heretic organization.
Cao Xuedong	New cultural trends	(a) Actively disseminate to the people the party's general and specific policies, laws and law regulations; (b) Initiatively observe discipline and law; and (c) Help the party branch to conduct good political work in compliance with the thoughts of the people.
Gao Jianfu	Political participation	(a) Timely collect information and give feedback on the opinions and suggestions by the villagers for the decision making of the two committees; (b) Participate in the concerned big programmes and policies of anent village; and (c) Help the party branch to think of ways and solutions.
Tang Ada	Supervision and control	(a) Supervise the work of the village's party branch; (b) Control whether big programmes and policies are in accordance with the higher level party committees and requirements by the government; and (c) Participate in the examination of the rationality and validity of the financial handlings.

As outlined before and visible in the tables on the administrative structures of the village, many members of the party branch are concurrently members of the VC, heads of VGs and lead VC sub-working groups. Apparently, the local CCP branch and its members hold key positions in the local governance process of Mengzibang. Yet, they have been elected by the villagers and are thus legitimized by vote.

As party members, they fulfil however tasks apart from their duties as VC members and these tasks are to introduce and consolidate party policies in the village as well as to observe and safeguard social stability. This is important for two reasons :

(1) Pool and minimize dangerous developments of popular demands for a greater degree of political self-determination that might well question national policies and the CCP's rule.

(2) Since the more distant, and thus more unchecked, cadres are from the Central Government in Beijing, the higher is the potential for corruption, non-compliance with national guidelines and policies and hence damaging developments on the grassroots level that can and will stir anger, followed by resistance within the population and both harm the economic upturn of China as well as the power status of the CCP. An example at this point shall not be the seldom cases of forced demolition of houses of citizens for construction projects by local officials — in not few cases against the awareness or approval of the Central Government — followed often by low compensation and anger within the population against this arbitrariness that in reported cases even leads to self-inflammation by the desperate house owners.

In view of this internal mistrust, unwished developments, dangers and problems within the party and its branch, its compliance with the higher level authorities as well as the execution of policy work in the interests of the villagers are hence cross-checked by cadres within the branch assigned with the supervision of the branch office's work.

Apart from that, the enforcements of state policies and guidelines on family planning, projects and objectives of the party branch or regulations from the higher level authorities, such as the city government of Kunshan, find their way into the grassroots level units of villages, being promulgated on public pinboards at the village service centre and thus communicated to the villagers. A recent example for the latter is the implementation of stricter regulations to curb smoking in public facilities, such as government buildings, public transport stations, dance locals, Karaoke bars or restaurants, with which the city government of Kunshan follows a nationwide trend that began in early 2010 in larger metropolis like Shanghai.

Mass Organizations

There are also so called mass organizations (*quntuan*) for different activities such as outdoor playing, women issues and dancing. These are established by the CCP and are meant to build bridges to the people and communicate their thoughts and interests. In fact, the mass organizations pool different kinds of age and social groups and are an important tool for the party to understand and supervise the thoughts of the people. In Mengzibang there are five mass organizations all headed by members of the local party branch :

Table 2.9: Mass Organizations

Assembly/Group/Branch	*Name*	*Assignment*
Women's Representative Assembly	Xie Meiying	Group head
	Zou Lao	Organisational service
	Zhao Aimei	Labour skills
	Xie Yuying	Birth planning
	Zhu Laoying	Safeguarding work
Youth League Branch	Cao Xuedong	Secretary
	Xie Qiaoquan	Member
	Gao Zhendong	Member
People's Militia Battalion	Cao Xuedong	Battalion Commander
	Zou Xin'gen	Political Instructor
Elderly People Association	Zhao Aimei	Head of Association
	Xu Aqiao	Member
	Cheng Yin'gen	Member
Handicapped People Association	Xu Fangming	Association President
	Zhao Aimei	Member
	Xu Aqiao	Member

Policy Control and Transparency : The Freedom of Determining Governance

Asked about the major challenges of in the administration of his village, the village leader specified the balancing of internal issues and discussions as the major challenge within the VC. During their regular meetings, decisions and voting within the VC are usually carried out by raising hands. In high compliance with the governance transparency stipulations of the OLVC and the JSLE, the administration of Mengzibang regularly publishes information on current economic plans, projects, financial *status quo* as well as name lists of all people involved in the administration of the village, such as the members from the VC, working groups, the local party branch, villagers representatives and staff workers. All these informations are made available to the public at the Village Service Centre.

In addition to the transparency requirement, there are two additional organs in Mengzibang to check the VC and its work, the Publicity Inspection Group (*gongkai jiandu xiaozu*) with seven members including one head, and the Democratic Financial Management Group (*minzhu licai xiaozu*) with five members including one head. The representatives of these two small groups are elected through the VRA and are the respective control organs in their working fields. In the case of the latter group, financial issues such as salaries, contracts and receipts are checked and verified in order to avoid fraud and corruption.

Table 2.10 : The Small Groups

Group	*Name*	*VC member/CCP member*
Publicity Inspection Group	Tang Ada (head)	No/Yes
	Xie Axing	No/Yes
	Chen Asan	No/Yes
	Zhao Taosheng	No/Yes
	Gong Peigen	No/Yes
	Zou Axin	No/NA
	Xiao Genfu	No/NA
Democratic Financial Management Group	Zhang Xulong (head)	Yes/Yes
	Xie Axing	No/Yes
	Chen Asan	No/Yes
	Zhao Taosheng	No/Yes
	Gong Peigen	No/Yes

In Mengzibang, however, these two important control groups overwhelmingly consist of members of the local party branch and even one member of the VC. In view of the high representation of party branch members in the constitution of the VC, there is apparent high risk that the members of the small groups — and given the relatively high numbers per group

Table 2.11: Villagers' Democratic Influence on Local Governance

Patterns of determining local governance	*Constraints*
Conduction of free and fair elections with public vote counting and manipulation control by EC.	—
Villagers are eligible to vote for the nominally highest self-administration unit (the VC).	Practically, the party secretary of the local party branch is more powerful and influential than the VC head, so the people do not elect the ultimate authority in the village.
The elected VC represents the interests of the villagers.	Mostly yes, but when these interests collide with the party secretary or the county-level authority, the powers of the VC are also constrained. The village administration is legally bound to support the county-level authorities to implement their policies, even unpopular ones like birth control or smoking prohibition.
The VRA convenes regularly and supervises, controls and evaluates the work of the VC.	In Mengzibang, many members of the VRA are concurrently party members and/or members of the VC, putting the impartiality of the VRA into question.
Speeches by candidates and subsequent questioning by the voters allowed.	—
Villagers may recall VC members if doubting their integrity (criminal offensces, corruption, etc.)	Over 1/5 of the villagers must accord to file a written complaint and substantiate reasons for the recall.
Work of the VC and particularly financial affairs of the village must be regularly published, enabling control by the villagers	—
Work of the VC is checked by small control groups, which are elected by the VRA.	VRA in Mengzibang predominantly consists of party branch/VC members; small control groups also filled with party branch/VC members.
Villagers can voice needs regarding economic and infrastructural improvements in the village.	Yet the final decision is made by the VC in accordance with the higher level authorities.

to curb potential intra-party dissenters — will not fully carry out their control duties in order to safeguard the integrity and reputation of the VC and likewise that of local party branch. Horizontally compared, the major patterns of democratic freedom to determine village governance and their constraints are given in Table 2.11:

Overall, the quality and degree of democratic freedom of the villagers to determine local governance lacks behind formal standard requirements in Western democracies, yet there has been much progress in China in the past years, particularly mirrored in the institutionalization of elections at the village level.

Projects and Innovative Activities

In line with the national government's objective of "building the new socialist village and a harmonic society", the village administration is actively pursuing a continuous improvement of the local living standard and quality and as such pursues a range of projects to facilitate life for the villagers. Projects and objectives of the local village administrations in the past three years were :

Infrastructural Goals

- construction of a 800 metres long, 7metres wide pathway;
- construction of a new bridge to West Mengzibang;
- construction of a public toilet in Gemu;
- fortification of 150 metres of pathway within the village; and
- construction of a Village Society Service Centre; and

- construction of a parking place close to the Village Society Service Centre.

Other Goals

- 85 per cent of all villagers shall by 2010 master a certain craft/skill;
- achieve an employment rate of 95 per cent;
- attain an animal/plant husbandry rate among 75 per cent of all village households;
- develop Gemu part of Mengzibang; and
- promote a greener more environmental-friendly village.

Photograph 2.16: Front Gate to the Village's Public Service Centre

The village leader stated that all of these goals were successfully achieved. As a result, Mengzibang has — as being shown in the pictures — since 2010, the already mentioned public service centre which houses the major administrative units, such as the VC, a village level military administration unit, the united working committee for companies and the branch office of the CCP. The major economic objectives for the current period focus on the integration of Mengzibang's growth with the development pace of the township level and on the attraction of more foreign investors to build factories and create more jobs in Mengzibang.

Finances

Although no detailed financial figures are available, the Village Leader provided some statistical information on the distribution of incomes and expenses by the village administration. The annual income of the Mengzibang administration is constituted by tax revenues and the renting out of public property apartments and buildings. 15 per cent of the annual outlays are reserved for the fishery industry. With more than 60 per cent, the largest share of expenses is — in an effort to follow the national objective of establishing a common social security system — attributed to the funding of the pensions of the retired villagers. The rest of the expenses is spent for the salaries of the public officers, public projects and other small social programmes. For the few comparably poorer villagers, the VC of Mengzibang arranges by the end of every year 500 RMB. This amount is arranged because — as the Village Leader simply explained during the interview — "illness leads to difficulties".

According to the duration of its administrative period, the VC usually lays out its plans in Three-Year steps. For the ninth legislature period between 2008 and 2010 the economic and financial goals of the VC were :

- 2008 : To achieve a total annual income of over 800,000 Renminbi (RMB) for the village and an average income per villager of annually 10,000 RMB;

- 2009 : To achieve a total annual income of over 900,000 Renminbi (RMB) for the village and an average income per villager of annually 12,000 RMB; and
- 2010 : To achieve a total annual income of over 1,020,000 Renminbi (RMB) for the village, a collective economic contracted income of 1,120,000 RMB and an average income per villager of annually 15,000 RMB; and
- To set up funds of annual 52,000 RMB for supporting poor people.

Reviewing the major economic achievements of the village, the village leader pointed particularly to the construction of two floor-level buildings in the 1980s and later on villas as well as to the achievement of a comfortable living standard (*xiaokang shuiping*) among the villagers. In the long term future perspective, he envisions a very prosperous Mengzibang with a wealthy living standard among the villagers.

Cultural and Livelihood Engagement of the People

Public Functions

Public functions are mainly organized by the local VC, the mass organizations in the village or also the local party branch, the latter with a big event in the village hall to celebrate the 90th Anniversary of the founding of the Chinese Communist Party. The nature of these public facilities is not only to interact with the villagers and accord their needs and requirements with the administration's policy plans, but also to supervise and study the villagers and propagate national and party policies.

Leisure Time Activities

While visiting Mengzibang, one particular leisure time and weekend enjoyment of the locals was apparent: playing Mahjongg (*majiang*), an ancient and throughout history very popular Chinese board game that also spread its fame to neighbouring Asian countries like Japan and Korea as well as to the West. In Mengzibang, there are several Mahjongg rooms, mostly attached on the backside of a small shop. There is also a public board game-room close to the Public Service Centre where people can gather to play. Particularly male locals meet up in their free time and play. The free time activities of females are traditionally rather constrained to the household and watching TV, take care of the children or also the meeting and talking with friends.

Photograph 2.17: Villagers Playing Mahjongg

Festivals and Religious Celebrations

The most important annual festival throughout China — and as such also in Mengzibang — is the Chinese New Year Festival (or Spring Festival) in January or February of the Gregorian calendar. It is for most Chinese families nowadays one of the very few occasions when the whole family is together and celebrates the beginning of the Chinese new year. Particularly regarding the rural area, following the massive economic upturn of the East Asian country in recent years many parents are separated from their children who search for work in the large but distant cities, sometimes more than a dozen hours by train away from home with seldom possibilities to return back. It is, therefore, not surprising that around the festivities of the Chinese New Year, when many employees are granted at least one to two weeks of home leave, trains, and buses and to a lesser degree airplanes get crowded. If not booking early, it is tremendously hard to obtain tickets in that time and the traffic infrastructure during these days is nearly about to collapse.

Further important festivals in the People's Republic of China are Labour Day on 1st May and the establishment of the PRC on 1st October — all celebrated in Mengzibang, too. Traditional cultural activities in Mengzibang celebrated during the Spring Festival include lion-dance (*wushi*), flower basket sluing-dance (*tiao hualan*) and *da lianxiang*, a type of dance performance, which is a local speciality of Mengzibang. Moreover, there are various cultural and artistic activities in Mengzibang apart from the common national festivals, ranging from spontaneous literature and art performances, traditional Chinese opera performances, dances and manifold recreation activities. Important venue for many of these activities is the local theatre hall. For religious celebrations, the village has a small temple where for example on New Year's Day incense is burnt and people pray, but many families also have a small shrine at home where gods are worshipped.

Marriage Functions

Many marriages in rural China take place in the course of the ceremony traditionally in the private home of the groom which is no different for Mengzibang. While visiting the village, a large wedding ceremony took place that was not only typical for its traditional local connotations, such as its celebration in the household of the groom, the decoration or the arranging of large food banquets, but also for the generosity and hospitability of the Chinese people towards foreign visitors. Right after arrival, the author was immediately invited to take part in the wedding, sit on a table and eat as he pleased. A personal highlight was the meeting with the groom and the bride and congratulating them to their wedding for which they happily and proudly guided the author to the newly furnished apartment. While guests for example in Iran are a

Photograph 2.18: Wedding in Mengzibang — Left: Entrance to the Venue and Right: Delicious and Abundant Food

valuable gift from god and treated in that way, in China they are — particularly foreigners — a source of internationality, fame and luck for the newly married and thus similarly very welcomed. This is even truer for rural China (Fig. 2.21).

Conflicts and Major Issues

As in any place of the world, there are also conflicts in a village such as Mengzibang which for outsiders are not easy to inquire and find out. A rare personal glimpse in this regard was the talk with a villager in a small shop, who complained that while VC claims the achievement of a comfortable standard of living, he himself would not feel much about it and sarcastically explained that if this was true they should give him money to help him overcome his financial struggle. Usually, Chinese prefer to solve conflicts and problems not in the public by screaming around, but in the closed and hidden backdoors to avoid that anyone of the involved loses his face. Face-saving and compromising of all stakeholders of a conflict is a very important aspect in Chinese culture that shall in no way be underestimated. Yet of course, there are everyday exceptions, particularly in cases when sensitive red lines are crossed. For the solution of conflicts in Mengzibang there is a mediation room close to the public service centre and the police station, where disputants behind closed doors solve their problems with the help of one or more mediators. As it has already been shown there are related civil mediation working committees both within the VC and the local party branch.

In contemporary China, thus also a Mengzibang, a major issue is that of distribution and ownership of land. The distribution of farmland is mainly carried out by the VC of Mengzibang. While nowadays there are farmland stock cooperatives with 19 contract households, originally land was distributed per person with 600 to 800 RMB per Mu. The construction of houses is normally subject to the scope of the builders, but may nevertheless not disturb the neighbours or block door entrances. Renovations of houses are in terms of possible issues of disturbance subject to discussion between involved people.

Concluding Remarks

Concluding remarks at this place cannot speak for the whole of China, which on the paper appears to be a unitary state, yet further down to the village level, the non-uniform characteristics of governance become visible. As such, since the various provincial legislations on village elections vary in terms of organizational and structural patterns of the election process as well the degree of democratic freedom, we explicitly refer to this case study of Mengzibang within the legal framework of local governance in Jiangsu province.

As compared to decades before, rural China and its villages have truly gained a higher degree of democratically constituted self-administration. Elections in the still rather authoritarian state have become institutionalized characteristics anywhere, allowing the villagers to determine their leaders to handle local affairs. For the CCP, village elections are a welcome win-win tool to both signalize the democratic aspects of the party and at the same time to have local cadres and officials checked upon the diligent fulfilment of their duties and thus strengthen top-down administrative control. But, the creationary powers of the village administration in Mengzibang to decide things faces several limits which are particularly geared to the complicated relationship between the democratically elected VC as administrative organ and the CCP branch as local party organ: with the leadership of the CCP constitutionally anchored in the People's Republic of China, the party organ is legally attributed more power than its administrative counterpart. As such, the villagers vote for an organ whose creationary powers are in theory constrained by potential interventions of the local party branch. In praxis, the extent of these interventions varies from village to village. Yet in Mengzibang, the high percentage of CCP party branch members in the current VC, thus being also democratically legitimized, suggest less potential conflict and are underlined by the satisfaction about steady economic and infrastructural progress and growth of welfare in the village, which were unanimously pointed out by almost all interviewed villagers.

Nevertheless, the local administration as representative of the interests of Mengzibang is an institutional counterweight against potential arbitrariness by local cadres. In this regard, apart from transparency and mutual performance checking, it has the power to intervene against meddling of the township authorities in the local self-administration by complaining at the higher level county authorities. The small control groups also have the potential to ensure the integrity of the work of the local administration, yet in the case of Mengzibang it is heavily entangled by biased members.

Given the rather low percentage of female actors in the village administration and the VC's obligation of implementing the widely unpopular national birth control policy, of which the guidelines and regulations are extensively published outside of the village service centre, the pro-women nature of the village administration is to be doubted. Although there is the party-founded Women's Representative Assembly and discrimination against the nation's "half the sky" is legally prohibited, male domination is still mirrored in the scarce election and placing of women into administrative posts or even into higher positions of administration, be it the VC, the VRA or the VG. Much more, the administration of Mengzibang takes care about the needs and problems of the poor and the village's environment. The VC does not only provide 500 RMB to all comparatively poorer people in the village, but also sets up annual funds for supporting poor, ill and disabled people that cannot help themselves financially. This fund is also increased annually. Likewise, green projects and incentives to protect the environment and thus save the natural resources of the village are also pillars of the local administration's work outlined the projects and plans for a greener and more environmental-friendly Mengzibang for the coming years. In this regard it can be said that the local administration is pro-poor and pro-environment.

REFERENCES

1. Hong Kong, a former British colony, was given back to the People's Republic in July 1997 while Macao, a former Portuguese colony, returned under jurisdiction of the PRC in December 1999.
2. Taiwan and several surrounding islands are currently under control of the 1949 exiled Republic of China (ROC).
3. The provisional capital city of the ROC in Taiwan is Taipei.
4. Cited from the records on Qin Shi Huang from the sixth annals of the Chinese dynastic histories in the Historical Records (Shi Ji) by Sima Qian *ca.* 163 - 85 B.C.) in Wang (2011), pp. 28-29.
5. For preparation of wars and conflicts, there was a further, military subdivision below county level into (in order): *xiang*, *ting*, *li*, *shi* and *wu*. The units are qualified as follows: one *wu*

consists of five households, one *shi* comprises two *wu*, one *li* constitutes ten *shi*, five *li* are a shortt*ing* (*duan ting*), ten *li* are a long *ting* (*chang ting*), ten *ting* are one *xiang* and one hundred *li* one *xian*; Xiao (2007).

6. Tan (2000), p. 29.
7. Xiong (2007), p. 61.
8. Duara (1988), p. 109.
9. Xiao (1967), p. 70.
10. Li (2005), pp. 41 - 42.
11. *Ibid.*, pp. 42– 43.
12. Wong (1997), p. 317.
13. Li (2005), p. 284.
14. Wong (1997), p. 317.
15. Li (2005), p. 8.
16. Duara (1988), pp. 42 – 46.
17. Wright and Duara list examples of heavy tax burden on the peasantry imposed by regional warlords and the GMD government that arose much discontent in rural China and strengthened the power base of the Chinese communists. *See* Wright (1951), p. 256 and Duara (1988), p. 178 and p. 191.
18. When Chiang Kai-Shek on 25 June, 1926 became Generalissimo of the National Revolutionary Army, he launched one month later on 27 July the Northern Expedition, which was a military undertaking to reunify China, combating against 'separatist' warlords.
19. Spence (1995), pp. 444 – 446.
20. Xiong (2007), pp. 62 – 63.
21. Duara (1988), pp. 223 – 224.
22. *Ibid.*, p. 224.
23. Wright (1951), p. 256.
24. Schurmann (1968), p. 431.
25. Lin (1990), pp. 1230 – 1231.
26. Xiong (2007), p. 63.
27. Schurmann (1968), p. 438.

28. Lin (1990), p. 1230.
29. The MATs were one of three major forms of cooperatives with which the CCP experimented in the early 1950s. In a MAT usually four or five households pooled their farm land, manpower, farming tools, seeds and animals. Further experimental cooperatives were the "elementary cooperative", pooling 20 – 30 households, and the "advanced cooperative", a collective farm. *Ibid.*, p. 1231.
30. MacFarquhar (1997), p. 57.
31. Lin (1990), p. 1233.
32. MacFarquhar (1997), p. 63.
33. Lin (1990), p. 1234.
34. *Ibid.*, p. 1234.
35. MacFarquhar (1997), pp. 95 – 96.
36. Lin (1990), pp. 1234 – 1235.
37. Zha (2005), p. 39.
38. Lin (1988), p. 199.
39. *See* for an analysis of the different figures on agricultural output in the 1980s: Lin (1990), pp. 1244 – 1247.
40. Alpermann (2005), p. 67.
41. Choate (1997), p. 5.
42. Alpermann (2005), p. 68.
43. The National People's Congress is the highest state body in the PRC.
44. Wang/Yao (2007), p. 1637.
45. Alpermann (2005), p. 69.
46. *Ibid.*, pp. 69 – 70.
47. Wang/Yao (2007), p. 1637
48. *Ibid.*, pp. 74 – 75.
49. Quanguo renmin daibiao dahui (2009).
50. Zhonghua renming gongheguo zhongyang renmin zhengfu (2010b).
51. The actual Constitution of the PRC was promulgated on the

Fifth Meeting of the Fifth's People's Congress on 4th December, 1982. The fourth and latest amendment of the Constitution was promulgated on the Second Meeting of the Tenth's People's Congress on 14th March, 2004. Throughout the text we will constantly refer to the latter.

52. Zhonghua renming gongheguo zhongyang renmin zhengfu (2010a).
53. Organisation for Economic Co-operation and Development (OECD) (2009), *op. cit.*, p. 119.
54. *Ibid.*, *op. cit.*, pp. 119 – 120.
55. Xiong (2007), *op. cit.*, p. 61.
56. Zhonghua renming gongheguo zhongyang renming zhengfu (2010a).
57. *Ibid.*
58. It is noted here that in terms of the village elections, the national legislation only lays down general principles that are interpreted and implemented differently in the 31 province-level units of the PRC. Chapter V will provide a detailed analysis of the provincial legislation for village elections for the Chinese case-study village Mengzibang in Jiangsu province. For a general overview and horizontal comparison of the varying provincial legislations on village elections *see* Alpermann (2007).
59. *See* section 'Systemic weaknesses and specialities of village governance in the PRC'.
60. Alpermann (2007), p. 2.
61. The Northern Song Dynasty is denominated Southern Song Dynasty after it moved its capital in 1127. It ruled until 1276.
62. Gaozong is the dynastical temple name for the Southern Song Dynasty's first emperor who was born as Zhao Gou.
63. Chinese unit. One mu equates to one sixth of an acre.

NOTES

Alpermann, Björn (2005), 'Grassroots Political Reforms in Rural

China', in: Schafferer, Christian (ed.): *Understanding Modern East Asian Politics*. New York: Nova Science Publishers, pp. 65-81.

Alpermann, Björn (2007), 'Provincial Legislation on Village Elections', in: *Zeitschrift für Chinesisches Recht*, 1 (14), pp. 1 – 26.

Choate, Allen C. (1997), 'Local Governance in China: An Assessment of Villagers Committees', in: *The Asia Foundation Working Paper Series*, 1 (February).

Duara, Prasenjit (1988), *Culture, Power, and the State: Rural North China, 1900-1942*.

Li Huaiyin (2005), *Village Governance in North China, 1875-1936*. Stanford: Stanford University Press.

Lin, Justin Yifu (1988), 'The Household Responsibility System in China's Agricultural Reform: A Theoretical and Empirical Study', in: *Economic Development and Cultural Change*, 36(3), pp. 199 – 224.

Lin, Justin Yifu (1990), 'Collectivization and China's Agricultural Crisis in 1959 – 1961', in: *Journal of Political Economy*, 98 (6), pp. 1228 – 1252.

MacFarquhar, Roderick (1997), *The Politics of China: The Eras of Mao and Deng*. Cambridge: Cambridge University Press.

Nanjingshi jiangningqu minzhengju - falü fagui jiansuo xitong [Civil Affairs Bureau of Jiangning District of Nanjing - Law and Regulation Searching Guide] (2000), *Jiangsu sheng cunmin weiyuanhui xuanju banfa* [Legislation for elections to the Villagers' Committee in Jiangsu Province]. Online:

http://www.jnqmzj.gov.cn/law/show.aspx?id=466&cid=21 (accessed: 27 October 2011)

Organisation for Economic Co-operation and Development (OECD) (2009), 'China', in: *OECD Rural Policy Reviews*. Paris: OECD.

Quanguo renmin daibiao dahui [National People's Congress (NPC)] (2009), 'Cunmin weiyuanhui zuzhifa (xiuding cao'an) tiaowen ji cao'an shuoming [Organic Law on Villagers Committees (revised draft) clauses and explanation of the draft], in: *Quanguo renmin daibiao dahui website*.

Schurmann, Franz (1968), *Ideology and Organization in Communist China*. Berkeley: University of California Press

Sima Qian (91 B.C.), Shi Ji: Qin Shi Huang benji diliu [The historical records: The sixth dynastical annals - Qin Shi Huang] in: Wang Shilin (2011), *Shi Ji*. Changchun. Jilin daxue chubanshe, pp. 26 – 38.

Spence, Jonathan D. (1995), *China's Weg in die Moderne*. Munich: DTV

Stanford: Stanford University Press.

Tan Qixiang (2000), 'Zhongguo lidai zhengqu gaishu' [Overview of the administrative divisions of China's past dynasties], in: *Changshui cuibian*. Shijiazhuang: Hebei jiaoyu chubanshe, pp. 23 -35.

Updated: 26 December 2009 (accessed: 11 July 2011)

Wong, Roy Bin (1997), 'Confucian Agendas for Material and Ideological Control in Modern China', in: Huters, Theodore; Wong, Roy Bin; Yu, Pauline (eds.): *Culture and State in Chinese History: Conventions, Accommodations, and Critiques*. Stanford: Stanford University Press, pp. 303 – 325.

Wright, Mary C. (1951), 'The Chinese Peasant and Communism', in: *Pacific Affairs*, 24 (3), pp. 256 – 265.

Xiao Gongquan (1967), *Rural China: Imperial Control in the Nineteenth Century*, Seattle: University of Washington Press.

Xiao Xi (2007), 'Kaijiang pitu shichuang zhongyang jiquan (tu) [Expanding the national territory and creating a centralized government (Picture)]', in: *Zhongguo wang* [China.com.cn], 27 August 2007. Online: http://big5.china.com.cn/aboutchina/zhuanti/lddw/2007-8/27/content_8750042.htm (accessed: 29 June 2011)

Xiong Wansheng (2007), 'Jiceng xingzhengquhua de guanli fudu yanbian: gulv yu qi - dui yi ge xian 150 nian quhua yanbian de zongguanxing yanjiu' [Transformation of the administration scope of grassroots administrative division: laws and inspirations – a thorough study on the transformation of 150 years of administrative division of a county], in: *Shanghai xingzheng xueyuan xuebao*, 8 (4), pp. 60 – 68.

Zha Daojiong (2005), 'China's Energy Security and Its International Relations', in: *The China and Eurasia Forum Quarterly*, 3 (3), pp. 39 – 54. Online: http://www.silkroadstudies.org/new/docs/CEF/Quarterly/November_2005/Zha_Daojiong.pdf (accessed: 8 July 2011)

Zhonghua renmin gongheguo zhongyang renmin zhengfu [Central People's Government of the People's Republic of China] (2010b), *Zhonghua renmin Gongheguo cunmin weiyuanhui zuzhifa* [Organic Law on Villagers Committees of the People's Republic of China]. Online: http://www.gov.cn/flfg/2010-10/28/content_1732986.htm (accessed: 11 July, 2011)

Zhonghua renming gongheguo zhongyang renmin zhengfu [Central People's Government of the People's Republic of China] (2010a), *Zhonghua renmin gongheguo xianfa* [Constitution of the People's Republic of China]. Online: http://www.gov.cn/gongbao/content/2004/content_62714.htm (accessed: 4 July 2011)

Zhonghua renming gongheguo zhongyang renmin zhengfu [Central People's Government of the People's Republic of China] (2010b), *Zhonghua renmin gongheguo xianfa* [Constitution of the People's Republic of China]. Online: http://www.gov.cn/gongbao/content/2004/content 62714.htm (accessed: 4 July 2011)

III

Rural Local Governance in India : Akathethara Grama Panchayat

Kerala is truly "God's Own Country". It is a beautiful green silver land. Coconut palms dominate the landscape. Kerala has a place of its own in the history of the world. Traditionally Kerala extended from Gokarnam (now in South Karnataka) to Kanyakumari (now in Tamil Nadu), but now confined to Malayalam speaking areas only. It is a narrow strip of coastal areas bounded by the Western Ghats on the one side and by the Arabian Sea on the other.

Because of its unique geographic position, it acted as a meeting place for many people, many religions, many ideas and ideologies. Travellers, merchants and rulers visited and influenced the history of Kerala. It is the story of a complex society with Indian outlook and open to West Asian influence. Kerala's unique selling point is its rich culture.

The recent history of Kerala includes the prelude to independence, the road to communism and the evolution of modern State of Kerala. Kerala developed a unique and distinctive culture. In art, thought, architecture, dress, social practices, crafts, beliefs, rituals, combat techniques, medicine indeed in every aspect of life. The culture evolved was both sophisticated and special.

The synonym associated with Kerala today is the Kerala Model of Development which is made possible with the efforts across the centuries. The story of modern Kerala and its transformation to a model State that most part of the third world asked to emulate.

The series of changes in the nineteenth century and early twentieth century developed the economic and social set-up of this region towards modernisation. Education with English as a component also began to spread around this time. This influenced by European ideas of equality and liberty and so began to acquire a skill that he could sell themselves to anyone who is willing to pay. The Kerala diaspora was due to the contact with foreign nations and literacy. The increase of literacy, books, newspapers and the ideas they spread transformed the people into the most politically active and right conscious in India. The investment made in health care and public distribution system also paid off.

The deep rooted caste hierarchy and its inhuman practices were prevailed in Kerala. Social reformers like Sree Narayana Guru strove to eradicate the practices. Along with Hinduism there existed Christianity and Islam in the Kerala society. In earlier times there was a strong presence of Buddhism and Jainism which also paved way for many good practices and their contribution to education and better life was also of importance. All these religions coexisted in Kerala without any communal conflicts. This mutual interaction helped to set in a process of cultural synthesis and social assimilation and moulded the Kerala society into a cosmopolitan one.

The Christian missionaries were the pioneers in Western education in Kerala. Politics, education, agitations, government action and the mass media have contributed to the integration of Kerala as apolitical system. Paradoxically, the average citizen is individualist, independent, and anarchic yet identifies themselves with the groups', viz., Extended family, village, caste, party, etc.

Women of Kerala from early days enjoyed to a large extent the liberty to live an outdoor life and they used this freedom judicially. Women in Kerala occupy high positions in every field of public sphere — medicine, engineering, law, etc. The social indicators like female life expectancy, MMR, IMR, sex ratio, etc., is indeed glorifying, but in real life situation is debatable.

The matriarchal system of inheritance existed among the major castes among Hindus viz. Ezhava and Nair communities till the beginning of the twentieth century. This helped women in controlling the assets and people consider them in high esteem. Now with the advent of modern social structure the joint family system which was prevalent among Keralites also disappeared and nuclear family is the fashion of the day. Still people are keeping their family bonds close to their heart.

I. Background

Akathethara is a Grama Panchayat coming under the Malampuzha Block of Palakkad District. It is situated on the lap of the Western Ghats. The entire Panchayat and the neighbouring areas including the Malampuzha dam were once under the control of Emoor Devaswom (Kallekulangara Hemambika Devi Temple). Legend says that the Malabar Coast was protected by the four Mother Goddesses, viz., Mookambika of Kolloor (North), Devi of Kodungalloor (West), Devi of Panachikavu (South) and Hemambika of

Photograph 3.1: Landscape of Kerala

Kallekulangara-Emoor (East). The idol worshipped at the Hemambika temple is the two hands of Devi, and local people remember with respect the visit of Smt. Indira Gandhi to the temple before adopting 'Hand' as her election symbol.

Basic Facts

The Panchayat consists of two revenue villages, namely, Akathethara and Puthupariyaram. It is under the Palakkad

Taluk. Akathethara Grama Panchayat consists of two Block Panchayat Divisions, viz., Akathethara and Malampuzha. The concerned District Panchayat Division is Puthupariyaram. It comes under the Malampuzha Assembly constituency which is now represented by Leader of the Opposition Sri. V.S. Achuthanandan, and the Parliament segment is represented by Sri M.B. Rajesh.

The population of the Panchayat as per 2001 Census is 25,458 (12,999 females and 12,459 males). Female population outnumbers that of the male. There are 1029 females for every 1,000 males.

Table 3.1: Akathethara Grama Panchayat : Basic Details

		Population Details			
		Gender	Population	S C	S T
Wards	17				
Area	19.79 sq.km.				
Population	25458	Male	12459	1373	53
Density	1286	Female	12999	1446	55
Literacy	96%	Total	25458	2819	108
Households	6500				

Table 3.2: Economic Division

Category	*Main Agricultural Labour*	*Main Household Industry*	*Main Other Workers*	*Total Workers*
Male	340	324	5043	5707
Female	497	158	1478	2133
Total	837	482	6521	7840

Table 3.3: Distribution of Skills

Category	*Number of families*	*Persons involved*
Artisans	12	22
Carpenters	38	78
Blacksmiths	13	19

Photograph 3.2: Grama Panchayat Office

Table 3.4: Industrial Classification of Main Workers

Category	*Cultivators*	*AL*	*LFP*	*M&Q*	*MPSH*	*MPSOH*	*CT*	*TC*	*TSC*	*OS*
Male	366	896	110	63	169	445	215	626	1285	818
Female	90	974	30	53	84	55	16	65	222	462
Total	456	1870	140	116	253	500	231	691	1507	1280

Source: AL-Agricultural Labours; LFP-Livestock, Forestry, Fishing and Plantation Workers; M&Q-Mining and Quarrying; MPSH-Manufacturing, Processing, Servicing and Repair in Household Industry; MPSOH- Manufacturing, Processing, Servicing and Repair other than Household Industry; CT-Construction; TC-Trade and Commerce; TSC- Transport, Storage and Communication; OS- Other Services.

Table 3.5: Public Facilities: Educational Institutions

Category	*Lower Primary School*	*Upper Primary School*	*High School*	*Higher Secondary School*	*Kendriya Vidyalaya*	*Industrial Training Institute*	*Engineering College*
Govt.	0	2	1	0	1	0	0
Aided	2	0	0	2	0	0	1
Private	1	2	0	0	0	1	0
Total	4	4	1	2	1	1	1

Table 3.6: Hospitals

Category	*Allopathic*	*Doctors*	*Ayurveda*	*Doctors*	*Homoeo*	*Doctors*
Government PHC	1	1	1	1	1	1
Private Hospital	2	5	3	3	6	6
Total	3	6	0	4	0	7
Hospital Beds	223	—	—	—	—	—

Table 3.7: Water Supply

Domestic Connections	6000
Agricultural Connections	129
Industrial Connections	41
Commercial Connections	22
Public Taps	102

Table 3.8: Wells/Ponds/Streams/Irrigation Canals/Tube Wells

Category	*Wells*		*Ponds/Tanks*		*Streams*	*Irrigation canals*	*Tube wells*	
	Private	*Public*	*Private*	*Public*	*(in metre)*	*(in metre)*	*Private*	*Public*
Seasonal	258	12	21	3	7525	0	0	0
Perennial	526	21	37	7	6350	12300	101	16
Useless	17	3	2	1	0	0	0	0
Total	**801**	**36**	**60**	**11**	**13875**	**12300**	**101**	**16**

Table 3.9: Agriculture Infrastructure

Land Details		
Type of land	*Number of plots*	*Area in Cents*
Wet Plots	1478	125442
Dry Plots	4573	347469
Total	**6051**	**472911**

Table 3.10: Financial Institutions (Banks)

Category of Bank	*Name of Bank*	*Branches*
Nationalised Banks	Indian Bank	1
" "	Union Bank of India	1
Cooperative Bank	Akathethara Coop Bank	2
Private Banks	..	2

Communication Facilities

Roads — The Panchayat is well connected with roads, viz., National Highway, State Highway, PWD Roads, and Panchayat roads. Every habitat is connected by roads.

Telephone – BSNL has one telephone exchange and well connected throughout the Panchayat. Mobile connectivity of all companies is operating here, viz., Aircel, Airtel, BSNL, Idea, Reliance, Tata, Uninor and Videocon.

Table 3.11: Industries

Medium industries	3
Small Scale Industries	151
1. Agro Based SSI	27
2. Rubber Based SSI	2
3. Plastic Based SSI	0
4. Forest Based SSI	8
5. Animal Husbandry Based SSI	2
6. Textile Based SSI	21
7. Chemical Based SSI	0
8. Engineering Based SSI	23
9. Electronic Based SSI	5
10. Mineral Based SSI	1
11. Building Material Based SSI	16
12. Other SSIs	46

Table 3.12: Public Distribution System

Ration Shops	7
Ration Card Holders	6153
Maveli Stores (Civil Supply Department)	1
LPG Agency	1
LPG Connections	4171

Major Institutions

1. Railway Divisional Office
2. Divisional Forest Office
3. Indo-Swiss Farm, Livestock Department
4. NSS Engineering College

Community Halls

6 (3 public and 3 private)

Stadiums – Indoor -1; Outdoor -1 (both owned by Indian Railways)

Burial Grounds

All Hindus – 1
Caste Hindus – 1

II. Structure of Panchayat

9 women and 8 men were elected to the Panchayat. This was made possible with the reservation. No woman was elected from a general seat. The member from Ward 6 is a SC woman though it is not reserved for SC. Minimum educational qualification is SSLC and maximum is Degree. Nine out of seventeen members have no real job. The political composition is not in favour of any political party. Both Congress and

Photograph 3.3: Smt. Valsala Chandran, President

CPI(M) got 8 seats each and with the support of the lone CPI member the CPM was able to gain power. Smt. Valsala Chandran of the CPI(M) is the President of the Panchayat. The average age of the members is less than 42 only.

Grama Sabha

Grama Sabhas have been given clear rights and responsibilities with absolute powers for identification of beneficiaries, powers for social audit and advisory powers for prioritising developmental needs.

Since the Panchayats in Kerala are having very big population, Grama Sabhas are conducted at Ward levels. Hence each Grama Panchayat has to conduct separate Grama Sabhas at each Ward. Minimum number of Grama Sabhas conducted in a year is two, and there are additional Grama Sabhas whenever it is necessary. It is mandatory on the part

Table 3.13: Details of the Grama Panchayat Ward Members

Ward	Name of member	Reser-vation*	Male/ Female	Age	Education	Work	Number of times elected	Party	Social Group
1.	K. Koyakutty	G	M	38	SSLC	Business	1st	Congress	Muslim
2.	C. Geetha	W	F	43	Degree	Social work	1st	CPI (M)	Hindu OBC
3.	V. Unnikrishnan	G	M	47	SSLC	Social work	1st	Congress	Hindu
4.	Valsala Chandran	W	F	52	SSLC	Social work	1st	CPI (M)	Hindu OBC
5.	K.K. Suresh Kumar	G	M	44	PDC	Clerk, Coop	2nd	CPI (M)	Hindu
6.	P. Lekshmi	W	F	41	PDC	LIC Agent	2nd	CPI	SC
7.	K. Satheesh	G	M	34	SSLC	Business	1st	Congress	Hindu OBC
8.	C. Prakashan	G	M	36	SSLC	Auto Driver	1st	Congress	Hindu OBC
9.	B. Santhosh	SC	M	30	SSLC	Social work	1st	CPI (M)	SC
10.	P. Udayakumari	W	F	45	SSLC	Clerk, Coop	1st	Congress	Hindu
11.	K.S. Udayakumara Menon	G	M	46	ITI	Surveyor	1st	CPI (M)	Hindu
12.	P. Parvathy	W	F	42	SSLC	House wife	1st	Congress	Hindu
13.	Sakunthala Vijayan	W	F	33	SSLC	Social Work	1st	CPI (M)	Hindu OBC
14.	K. Jayakrishnan	G	M	41	Degree	Govt Project	1st	CPI (M)	Hindu
15.	Smitha Alwin	W	F	44	SSLC	Social Work	1st	Congress	Hindu OBC
16.	Sumathi Mohan	W	F	50	SSLC	House Wife	1st	Congress	Hindu OBC
17.	V.V. Kamalakshi	SC-W	F	44	SSLC	Social Work	1st	CPI (M)	SC

* G — General W — Women SC — Scheduled Caste SCW — Scheduled Caste Women

Photograph 3.4: Grama Sabha

of the member of the Ward to conduct Grama Sabha in time, and the member will lose office if she/he cannot conduct it in time.

Grama Sabhas would be held after sufficient environment creation and information through the media as well as specifically through educational institutions, people's organisations, work places and NHG network. Six facilitators should be trained for each Grama Sabha with three women nominated by the NHG and one woman and two men identified unanimously by the Panchayat. The agenda should be semi-structured through a questionnaire covering key development issues within the Panchayat. Detailed discussions are to be held up in break-up groups.

With the help of the questionnaire and with the assistance of the facilitators, Grama Sabhas would be asked to list out priorities clearly ranked. In the case of infrastructure like roads, buildings, irrigation schemes, water supply schemes, electrification, the Grama Sabha should list out norms for prioritisation and then priorities for the whole Grama Panchayat. The intervention plan in agriculture, irrigation and environment shall be based on watershed plans. Suggestions on maintenance of assets would be recorded separately.

The following records of the Grama Sabha are collected and maintained by the Secretary of the Panchayat :

1. Photographs;
2. Attendance register showing details of house number, address, age, whether male or female, whether belonging to SC/ST, occupation, etc.;
3. Record of discussion of the Grama Sabha; and
4. Recommendations of the Grama Sabha.

Women Representation

As per the provisions of the Panchayati Raj Act, 50 per cent seats are reserved for women. Since the Panchayat is having 17 constituencies, 9 seats are reserved for women.

Mere representation may not do any good to the women at large, but it certainly will give them an opportunity to get acquaint with the functions of the Panchayat including planning and execution. In the case of Grama Sabha even without any reservation more than 60 per cent of the participants are women, but the real emancipation lies in whether they have any role in decision making or they are attending it just for the sake of attending. Here lies the crux of the issue. Women are attracted to the Grama Sabha because they are aware of the fact that it is the forum where beneficiaries for assistances are being selected and due to the compulsion from the members of the Panchayat as they consider women as silent participants. The very same thing happens in the Panchayat also. Since certain seats are reserved for women, the political parties were forced to find candidates for the reserved seats. Often the selection goes to family members of political party leaders itself. Whenever the reserved Ward is dereserved certainly a male candidate will contest from there. It would be better if the reservation will stay at least for two terms in a constituency, for enabling the women member to contest for a second term.

Representation of Marginalised Groups

Marginalised groups such as people belonging to Scheduled Caste are adequately represented in this Panchayat. Two seats were reserved for them, one SC open and another SC woman. But another SC woman candidate won from an unreserved constituency, which marks a good beginning. Even without any reservation, seven members elected belong to the OBC category among the Hindus. So altogether the weaker sections, i.e., SC, OBC and women got 11 seats out of 17 seats.

Grama Panchayat has four Standing Committees. The Standing Committees are constituted in such a way that every member of the Panchayat gets a chance to function in one Standing Committee or the other. Each Standing Committee is assigned certain subjects and these Committees are expected to go into the subject areas both at the planning and implementation stage in great detail. For the purpose of co-ordination, a Steering Committee is constituted consisting of the President and Vice President of the Panchayat and the Chairpersons of Standing Committees. In addition, there are Functional Committees for different subjects who can include experts and practitioners and the Panchayats are free to constitute Sub Committees to assist the Standing Committee or Functional Committee. There is also provision for constitution of Joint Committees with neighbouring Grama Panchayats.

Table 3.14: Committee System

Committee	Ward	Name of member
	4	Valsala Chandran (President)
Finance	5	K.K. Suresh Kumar (Vice President)
,,	1	K. Koyakutty
,,	9	B. Santhosh
,,	10	P. Udayakumari
,,	15	Smitha Alwin
Development	6	P. Lekshmi
,,	11	K.S. Udayakumara Menon
,,	16	Sumathi Mohan
Welfare	2	C. Geetha
,,	7	K. Satheesh
,,	13	Sakunthala Vijayan
,,	14	K. Jayakrishnan
Health and Education	3	V. Unnikrishnan
,,	8	C. Prakashan
,,	12	P. Parvathy
,,	17	V.V. Kamalakshmi

Elections to the Grama Panchayat

Kerala has one of the best Election Commission in the country with powers for absolute control over staff on election duty, preparation of voters list, verification of accounts and disqualification of candidates not submitting accounts in time, conduct of elections of the head of Grama Panchayats as well as to the District Planning Committees, conduct of no confidence motions and disqualification of defectors.

Under the Election Commission there is an independent Delimitation Committee to carry out delimitation of Wards.

Election is carried out every five years, and bye election to the seats which became vacant due to resignation, disqualification, death, etc., will be conducted within six months. Bye elections are conducted regularly to those vacant seats.

III. Functions assigned to Grama Panchayats

A. Mandatory Functions of Grama Panchayats

1. Regulation of building construction.
2. Protection of public land from encroachment.
3. Protection of traditional water sources.
4. Preservation of ponds and other waterbodies.
5. Maintenance of waterways and canals under their charge.
6. Collection and disposal of solid waste and control of liquid waste disposal.
7. Strom water drainage.
8. Maintenance of environmental hygiene.
9. Management of markets.
10. Vector control.
11. Regulation of slaughtering of animals and sale of meat, fish and other perishable food items.
12. Regulation of eating establishments.
13. Prevention of food adulteration.
14. Maintenance of roads and other public assets.
15. Street lighting and their maintenance.
16. Immunization.
17. Carrying into effect national and State level strategies and programmes for disease prevention and control.
18. Operating and maintenance of burial and burning grounds.
19. Licensing of dangerous and offensive trades.
20. Registration of births and deaths.

21. Providing bathing and washing ghats.
22. Providing ferries.
23. Provide parking space for vehicles.
24. Provide waiting sheds for travellers.
25. Provide toilet facilities in public places.
26. Regulate conduct of fairs and festivals.
27. Licensing of pet dogs and catching of stray dogs.

B. General Functions of Grama Panchayats

1. Collection and updating of essential statistics.
2. Organizing voluntary labour and contribution for community works.
3. Carrying out campaign for thrift.
4. Awareness building for control of social evils like drinking, consumption of narcotics, dowry and abuse of women and children.
5. Ensuring maximum people's participation in all stages of development.
6. Organizing relief during natural calamities.
7. Inculcating environmental awareness and motivating local action for environmental upgradation.
8. Promoting co-operatives.
9. Enhancing communal harmony.
10. Mobilizing local resources in cash and in kind, including free surrender of land for development purposes.
11. Spreading legal awareness among the weaker sections.
12. Campaigning against economic crimes.
13. Organizing neighbourhood groups and self-help groups with focus on the poor.
14. Awareness building on civic duties.

Preparation of Plan

Plan preparation is an important function assigned to the Grama Panchayat. Preparation of Plan is to be done meticulously. The following steps are involved in the preparation of Plan in a Grama Panchayat.

1. Situation analysis by mandatory working groups headed by a member of Panchayat and experts as members.
2. Pre Grama Sabha consultations with key stakeholders.
3. Holding of Grama Sabha.
4. Watershed planning.
5. Preparation of development report and vision document.
6. Draft Plan preparation.
7. Development seminar.
8. Reorientation by Grama Panhchayat.
9. Projectisation.
10. Plan finalization.
11. Plan vetting by Technical Advisory Group.
12. Approval by District Planning Committee (DPC).
13. Post approval steps.

IV. Responsibilities of Grama Panchayat

Developmental responsibilities are now transferred to Panchayats. In the case of infrastructure, barring Highways and major District Roads, connectivity became the responsibility of the Panchayats. In the case of power, in addition to the traditional function of street light maintenance, extension of electricity lines to unserviced areas is now by and large carried out by Panchayats. They also play a major role in promotion of non-conventional energy. Sanitation including solid and liquid waste management is now under Grama Panchayats. Rural water supply also comes under Grama Panchayats. Promotion of cottage and small industries is a shared responsibility.

In agriculture and allied services the following are the functions of the Grama Panchayats:

- Agricultural extension including farmer oriented support for increasing production and productivity.
- Watershed management and Minor Irrigation.
- Dairy Development.
- Animal Husbandry, including veterinary care.
- Inland Fisheries.

As regards Social Welfare, the entire functions except juvenile justice lie with Panchayats. ICDS is fully implemented by Panchayats. Care of disabled also to a greater level became the responsibility of Panchayats. In the field of Social Justice, 50 per cent of TSP and two-third of SCP is planned and implemented by Panchayats. Welfare pensions are administered by Panchayats, including selection of beneficiaries and disbursement of pension.

All Centrally Sponsored Anti-Poverty Programmes are planned and implemented by Panchayats. In the field of education, the responsibility is confined to primary school level. The public service institutions and officers related to these responsibilities are transferred to Panchayats, who have responsibility for:

- Routine maintenance.
- Upkeep and maintenance of equipments.
- Replenishment of consumables.

- Meeting of non-salary administrative charges.

Sector-wise Distribution of Responsibilities

(i) Agriculture

1. Bring into cultivation wasteland and marginal lands.
2. Bring about an optimum utilization of land.
3. Soil conservation.
4. Production of organic manure.
5. Establishment of nurseries.
6. Promotion of cooperative and group farming.
7. Organizing self help groups among cultivators.
8. Promotion of horticulture and vegetable cultivation.
9. Fodder development.
10. Plant protection.
11. Seed production.
12. Farm mechanization.
13. Management of Krishi Bhavans.

(ii) Animal Husbandry and Dairy

1. Cattle improvement programmes.
2. Dairy farming.
3. Poultry farming, bee keeping, piggery development, goat rearing, rabbit rearing.
4. Running of veterinary dispensaries.
5. Running of ICDP sub-centres.
6. Preventive health programmes for animals.
7. Prevention of cruelty to animals.
8. Fertility improvement programmes.
9. Control of disease of animal origin.

(iii) Minor Irrigation

1. All micro irrigation schemes.
2. Water conservation.

(iv) Fisheries

1. Development of fisheries in ponds and fresh water and brackish water fish culture, Mari culture.
2. Fish seed production and distribution.
3. Distribution of fishing implements.
4. Fish marketing assistance.
5. Provision of basic minimum services for the families of fishermen.
6. Welfare schemes for fishermen.

(v) Social Forestry

1. Rising of fodder, fuel and fruit trees.
2. Organizing campaigns for tree planting and environmental awareness.
3. Forestation of waste lands.

(vi) Small Scale Industries

1. Promotion of cottage and village industries.
2. Promotion of handicrafts.
3. Promotion of traditional and mini industries.

(vii) Housing

1. Identification of homeless people and *porompoke* (government land) dwellers and provide house sites and houses.

2. Implementation of rural housing programmes.
3. Implementation of shelter upgradation programmes.

(viii) Water Supply

1. Running of water supply schemes covering the entire Grama Panchayat.
2. Setting up of water supply schemes covering the Grama Panchayat.

(ix) Electricity and Energy

1. Street lighting.
2. Promotion of bio-gas.

(x) Education

1. Management of Government pre-primary schools and Government Primary Schools.
2. Literacy programmes.

(xi) Public Works

1. Construction and maintenance of village roads within the Grama Panchayat.
2. Construction of buildings for institutions transferred.

(xii) Public Health and Sanitation

1. Management of dispensaries and primary health centres (in all system of medicines).
2. Management of child welfare centres and maternity homes.
3. Immunization and other preventive measures.

4. Family welfare.
5. Sanitation.

(xiii) Social Welfare

1. Running of Anganwadis.
2. Sanctioning and distribution of pensions to destitute, widows, handicapped and agricultural labourers.
3. Sanctioning and distribution of unemployment allowance.
4. Sanctioning and assistance for marriage of the daughters of widows.
5. Management of group insurance scheme for the poor.

(xiv) Scheduled Castes and Scheduled Tribes Development

1. Beneficiary oriented schemes under SCP and TSP.
2. Management of nursery school for SC and ST.
3. Provision of basic amenities in SC and ST habitats.
4. Assistance to SC and ST students.
5. Discretionary assistance to SC and ST in need.

(xv) Sports and Cultural Affairs

Renovation of playgrounds

(xvi) Public Distribution System

1. Examination of complaints against the Public Distribution System and taking of remedial measures.
2. Organization of campaigns against weights and measures offences.
3. General supervision and guidance of ration shops and

Maveli stores and other public distribution centres and if necessary starting new public distribution centres.

(xvii) Natural Calamities Relief

1. Management of relief centres.
2. Organization of relief works.

(xviii) Co-operatives

1. Organization of co-operatives with in the jurisdiction of the Panchayat.
2. Payment of Government Grants and subsidies within the jurisdiction.

V. Activities of Grama Panchayat

Other than the Grama Panchayat office the following offices are also functioning under the Grama Panchayat.

1. Government Upper Primary School, Akathethara;
2. Government Upper Primary School, Ummini;
3. Krishi Bhavan, Akathethara, with Agriculture Officer;
4. Veterinary Hospital, Akathethara with Veterinary Surgeon;
5. Veterinary Sub Centre, Ummini;
6. Public Health Centre, Akathethara with Medical Officer;
7. Ayurveda Dispensary, Akathethara with Medical Officer;
8. Homoeo Dispensary with Medical Officer;
9. Assistant Engineer, Grama Panchayat;
10. Village Extension Officer; and
11. 26 Anganwadis and Supervisor.

Activities in Agriculture

Watershed Master Plan was prepared with the assistance of Integrated Rural Technology Centre (IRTC) and the same is being used as a primary document for all soil and water related activities. Planning by the Panchayat for developmental activities also is based on the watershed plan. Mahatma Gandhi NREGS works are also arranged according to the watershed plan for the benefit of the farmers and for sustainable agricultural activities.

There are a few committees functioning in the Panchayat for the agricultural activities, viz., Kera Samithy (Committee for Coconut), Padasekhara Samithy (Committee for paddy field), Neerthada Samithy (Watershed Committee), etc. The Panchayat took a lead role in convergence of the activities of all the related committees for better benefit for the farmers and sustainability to nature.

Modern agricultural implements were purchased by the Panchayat and made them available to the farmers at subsidised rate.

Shortage of agricultural labour is a major concern in the farming sector of Kerala, and to overcome this situation, a Labour Bank was formed and its members were trained and their service was ensured to the farmers.

Vermi-compost a by-product of the Solid Waste Plant functioning in the Panchayat is being given to the farmers at a subsidised rate.

- Crop insurance was given to all kinds of crops in the Panchayat.
- Vegetable cultivation was encouraged to make the Panchayat rely less on vegetables from Tamil Nadu.
- Rs. 2,500/ha was given as subsidy to farmers for

harvesting and interest free revolving fund was given to farmers for harvesting.

- Vermi compost units were given to individual homes.
- Pisciculture in fresh water started in 26 ponds. (15 acres)
- Data regarding agriculture and allied activities were given to farmers by utilising e-Krishi project.
- Fertilizers and pesticides were given free of cost to farmers.
- Procurement of rice at Rs. 12/kg was arranged through Supplyco. (Civil Supplies Department)
- MGNREGS activities were put to use for the benefit of farmers.
- Training of paddy, mushroom and vegetable cultivation were arranged throughout the Panchayat.

  N.B.— Income from agricultural output was increased from Rs. 88 lakh in 2008 to Rs. 112 lakh in 2009 (27% increase).

Activities in Health Sector

- New building for Ayurveda dispensary.
- Ensure service of Doctors and medicine at hospitals.
- Conducted medical camps in SC colonies.
- ASHA worker's service extended to all parts of Panchayat.
- Cancer detection camps conducted with the help of Regional Cancer Centre.
- Two sub-centres for Ayurveda dispensary started.
- Palliative care ensured for 73 persons by providing medicine, bed, etc., and ensure weekly visit to their residence on Tuesday.

- Special diabetics, cardiology and orthopaedic clinics every week at the PHC.
  N.B.—Health care became affordable to the public.

Activities in Animal Husbandry

- Veterinary clinic modernised.
- 177 high breed cows were distributed.
- Free veterinary check up in two sub-centres every week.
- 5,600 chicks were given for developing backyard farming. Milk chilling plant constructed by the Panchayat for milk societies in the Panchayat.
- Free insurance coverage for animals.
  N.B.—Panchayat became surplus in milk production and 58 per cent egg demand is being met internally.

Activities in Education Sector

- Rs. 2 lakh expended in two years.
- Computer provided for Government Upper Primary Schools.
- Maintenance work to Akathethara UP School.
- Baby friendly toilets in all schools.
- Drinking water facility to schools.
- Compound wall provided for schools.
- Bio-gas plant in two schools.
- Planting of trees by students at schools and homes.
- Education Samithy formed at Grama Panchayat level.
- Teachers' conventions at every month.
- Assessment of the level of improvement of students conducted every month.

- Diary given to all students for developing the habit of diary writing.
- Science, Literature and Maths camps conducted every year.
- Sports kits given to students.
- Parent-Teacher Association meetings conducted regularly.
- Extra classes given to students of 10th standard with supplementary food.

  N.B.—Pass percentage in government schools improved from 26 per cent to 82 per cent in two years.

Activities in Child Welfare

- 14 out of 26 Anganwadis got new building with Panchayat assistance.
- Land procured for another eight Anganwadis.
- Supplementary nutrition for adolescent girls.
- Employment training and counselling for girls.
- Conducted festivals for Anganwadis.
- Baby friendly toilets to Anganwadis.

Activities in Drinking Water Supply

- 20 rain water harvesting structures in various areas of Panchayat including schools and Anganwadis.
- Desilting of ponds increased water availability to the nearby wells.
- Domestic connections to SC habitats.

  N.B.—Water borne diseases controlled.

Activities in Eco Restoration

- 1.25 lakh saplings distributed for planting in public and private lands.
- Reclamation of 25 acres river side from private encroachers and bamboo cultivation on the river sides.
- Desilting of ponds with MGNREGA assistance.
- Four watersheds identified and master plan prepared.

  N.B.— Awareness created among the people on global warming and the need for protecting nature.

Activities in Women Sector

- 145 Kudumbasree units formed with 2,241 members.
- Training given to members for taking up economic activities.
- Participation of women in Solid Waste Management Project.
- Status of women improved with more financial independence to them.
- Subsidy for group economic activities from Panchayat for starting napkin manufacturing unit (Rs. 1.6 lakh)

  N.B.— Women empowerment in social, economic and political fields.

Activities in Power Sector

- CFL lamps distributed at Rs. 30/lamp.
- Free CFL lamp for Scheduled Caste/Scheduled Tribe families
- Street lights throughout the Panchayat
- Power line mapping conducted.

  N.B.—Panchayat became 100 per cent electrified.

Activities in Social Security Sector

- House for all in the Panchayat.
- Pension for unwedded ladies above 50 years (26 in number)
- Janasree Bima Yojana (LIC) for all MGNREGS workers.

Activities in Sanitation Sector

- Solid Waste Management project launched for handling 2 tonnes of bio degradable waste.
- Bins supplied to houses to collect waste at home.
- Special vehicle procured to transport waste from source to plant.
- Processed and disposed plastic waste.
- Toilet to all houses, schools and Anganwadis.
- Campaign to discourage use of plastic.

  N.B.—Panchayat received Nirmal Gram Puraskar from Government of India

Activities in Caring the Aged

- Ward level committees to monitor the condition of the aged.
- Pension arranged for all above 65 years.
- Food security, health security and financial security to elders.
- Survey conducted among the elders to find out their specific issues.
- Training given to elders on simple exercises.

  N.B.—From exclusion and agony to social inclusion.

Activities under MGNREGA

- Desilting and renovating traditional water sources like ponds and tanks.
- Desilting and renovating irrigation canals.
- Check dams and earthen bunds for soil and water conservation.
- Afforestation activities.
- Cleaning of drainages and there avoiding/reducing the menace of mosquitoes.
- Model social audit.
- Janasree Bhima Yojana Insurance coverage for 683 families.
- 90 per cent work by women.
- Bank account and savings for all.

  N.B.—Natural resource management, women empowerment.

Photograph 3.5: MGNREGA at work

Activities in Arts, Sports and Cultural Areas

- Panchayat level youth festival.
- Registration arranged to all sports clubs and reading rooms with Sports Council.

- Sports kits given to 17 clubs.
- Conducted football matches during the World Cup period.
- Training given to women in *chenda* (traditional drum instrument).
- Training given to boys and girls in swimming.

  N.B.—Involvement of youth in Panchayat activities.

Activities in Modernising Governance

- Citizens Charter published.
- Computerise the activities of the Panchayat.
- Front office established to deal with the public.
- Utility card given to all families.
- Transparent and corruption free administration.
- Attendance of all offices attached to the Panchayat is published.
- Facilitation centres for all offices.

  N.B.—People friendly office.

Photograph 3.6: Front Office

VI. Innovative Activities

1. Watershed Master Plan

A comprehensive master plan was prepared by the Grama Panchayat with the technical assistance of Integrated Rural Technology Centre (IRTC), Palakkad. The activities involved identification of four watersheds in the Panchayat, viz., Cheekuzhy watershed (829.43 ha.), Akathethara watershed (623.43 ha.), Cherad watershed (99.14 ha.) and Dhoni-Karippalathodu watershed (44.56 ha.). Present condition of the watershed is identified and interventions needed were also brought to the plan with the assistance of experts from Agriculture, Animal Husbandry, Soil Conservation, Soil Survey, Kerala Water Authority, Rural Development, Panchayat, etc. The Plan was vetted at the District level and it was placed before the District Planning Committee (DPC) and finally approved for implementation.

Photograph 3.7: Rain water collection Pits

Photograph 3.8: Watershed Management

NABARD is assisting the activities through the Watershed Committees formed for implementation and monitoring. Manpower needed for the activities are being channelised through Mahatma Gandhi NREGS and finance needed for material component is being met from NABARD assistance. Activities involved are rain water harvesting structures, bunds, gully plugging, rain pits and livelihood activities. Akathethara became the first Panchayat in Kerala to develop a Watershed Master Plan.

2. *Green the Gap Project*

Palakkad Gap is the biggest gap in the Western Ghats, and it acts as a link between Kerala and Tamil Nadu. It is 51km wide and it allows the dry wind from Eastern parts of Western Ghat (Tamil Nadu) to enter Kerala. Hence, Palakkad is experiencing the warmest climate in Kerala. Formerly the gap was filled with forest and it prevented the free flow of dry wind. With the deforestation the entire climate of Palakkad

Photograph 3.9: Planting Saplings at Wayside

became worse and Akathethara lies at the mouth of the Palakkad Gap and also experience the burnt of nature.

The Grama Panchayat comes out with a new scheme to give a green cover to the Akathethara region of Palakkad Gap. The project started with IEC activities and prominent environmentalists were roped into associate with the project. The following activities were undertaken:

- Conducted awareness camps among the school children, women NHGs, members of Reading Rooms and among the youths.
- Local varieties of plants were selected for planting.
- Seeds were collected from local mango trees, jackfruit trees and a variety of local grown trees through the school children.
- Seeds were grown up in selected nurseries with the assistance of women SHGs.
- 1.25 lakh saplings were distributed among the people for planting.

- Planting was done by the Panchayat as a festival involving all sectors of people.
- School children were entrusted with planting of saplings at the school as well as at their homes.
- Plants were protected and given water throughout the summer season through Mahatma Gandhi NREGS.

Over 80,000 plants survived and now that people mainly school children are continuing the work. The message preservation of nature and its environment to our survival was given to the coming generation. It was a first step in arresting Global Warming by a Grama Panchayat.

3. Solid Waste Management

Being a semi-urban Grama Panchayat, Akathethara faces the common problems being confronted by urban areas – that of sanitation. Akathethara is a Nirmal Panchayat with all houses having sanitary latrines, all schools having toilet facilities and all Anganwadis having baby friendly toilets. Personal hygiene is ensured. But hygiene at public places is very poor in all the populated areas of Kerala, and Akathethara is no exception.

The main source of waste in the Panchayat is domestic garbage which they used to dump in public places, which make life miserable for the common people. To address the issue the Panchayat had developed a decentralized solid waste management system based on environment friendly technologies. The technical advice was given by IRTC.

They have started a solid waste management plant in the Panchayat. Panchayat had provided bins for houses and kept bins at public places for collection of waste People were educated on the need for segregation of waste and the waste so segregated was collected at the bins. The same is transported to the plant by women SHG members using a three wheeler vehicle provided by the Panchayat. The plastic waste will be made to bundles and pressed them to make cakes so that they can be sold to plastic recycling units. The bio degradable waste will be treated in an organic way by utilizing the worms to generate vermin compost. Daily the unit is capable of handling two tonnes of waste.

The Panchayat is spending Rs. 4 lakh every year for maintaining the plant. The vermin compost is given to the farmers at subsidized rate. The earnings from vermin compost and plastic sale per year are around Rs. 40,000.

VII. Finance

Financial Handling at Grama Panchayat

The traditional sources of income available to Grama Panchayat can be classified into tax revenue and non-tax revenue.

Tax revenue is taxes directly demanded and collected by Grama Panchayats:

1. **Property Tax** — Property tax constitutes a major item of revenue for Grama Panchayats which has a per capita collection of Rs. 32. The plinth area based assessment is being practiced here.

   Residential - Rs. 3 to Rs. 8
   Industrial - Rs. 6 to Rs. 16
   Commercial - Rs. 12 to Rs. 64

   Panchayats have the freedom to fix the base rate between the minimum and maximum rates fixed by Government.

2. **Profession Tax** — It constitutes the Second largest source of own income to a Grama Panchayat. The slab is as follows (for Half Year income) :

Class I	Rs. 12,000 to Rs. 17,999	Rs. 120
Class II	Rs. 18,000 to Rs. 29,999	Rs. 180
Class III	Rs. 30,000 to Rs. 44,999	Rs. 300
Class IV	Rs. 45,000 to Rs. 59,999	Rs. 450
Class V	Rs. 60,000 to Rs. 74,999	Rs. 600
Class VI	Rs. 75,000 to Rs. 99,999	Rs. 750
Class VII	Rs. 1,00,000 to Rs. 1,24,999	Rs. 1,000
Class VIII	above Rs. 1,25,000	Rs. 1,250

3. **Entertainment Tax** — It provides the third largest source of income. It is fixed as 25 per cent of the price.
4. **Advertisement Tax** — It is having potential in the Kerala context but usually not collected. There is no minimum or mode of collection fixed by Government and left to Panchayats.
5. **Service Tax** — It is collected as a small tax.
6. **Show Tax** — It includes surcharges which can be collected on any entertainment, exhibition, performance, amusement game, sports or race.
7. **Cess on Conversion of Land Use** — It is a cess which can be levied by Panchayat for conversion of land use from paddy field, marshy land, pond or waterbody into garden or building site, but since severe restrictions are there on the conversion of land use, the collection of tax has been very low.
8. **Surcharges** — Panchayats are empowered to levy surcharges up to 5 per cent on the property tax subject to a maximum of two surcharges.

Non-Tax Revenue

Non-Tax Revenue of a Grama Panchayat is as follows :

1. *License Fee*
   (a) Trade licenses.
   (b) Licenses under Prevention of Food Adulteration Act.
   (c) Licensing of private slaughter houses.
   (d) Licensing of private markets.
   (e) Licenses under the Kerala Places of Public Resorts Act.
   (f) Licensing of private parking and halting places.
   (g) Licensing of private burial and burning places.
   (h) Licensing of Technical Experts.
   (i) Licensing of domestic animals.
   (j) Licensing of animal stalls kept for commercial places.
   (k) Licensing of special trades like butcher, fishmongers, poulterers, commission agents, brokers, etc.
2. *Gate Fee* — Normally Gate Fee is collected by auction to the highest bidder in a :
   (a) public market.
   (b) public parking/halting place.
   (c) public slaughter house.
3. *Income from Property (Rent)*
   (a) Rent from buildings.
   (b) Rent from land.
   (c) Rent from clock room and comfort stations.
4. *Income from property other than rent*
   (a) Proceeds from sale of right to collect river sand.

(b) Proceeds from sale of right to catch fish.
(c) Proceeds from sale of usufructs.

5. *Permit Fees, viz.*
   (a) Fee for building permits.
   (b) Fee for the construction, establishment or installation of factories, workshops or places where electricity is used.
6. *Registration Fees, viz.*
   (a) Registration of hospitals, and Para Medical institutions.
   (b) Registration of tutorials.
   (c) Registration of births and deaths.
   (d) Registration of lodgings.
7. *Service/Use Charges*
   It relates to charges collected for use of utilities and amenities provided by the Panchayat.
8. *Income from Ferries*
   Income from ferries can be collected either by auctioning or by collecting from users.
9. *Fines and Penalties*
   Fines and penalties can be realized when there is a contravention of regulations or there are belated payments.
10. *Sundry Items, viz.*
    (a) Proceeds from auctioning meat stalls.
    (b) Interest on deposits.
    (c) Endowments.
    (d) Return on investments like shares.
    (e) Contributions/donations.
    (f) Hire charges of vehicles/machinery.
    (g) Income from cattle pounds.
    (h) Income from libraries.

(i) Sale of forms.
(j) Sale of unserviceable articles and fallen trees.

Grants-in-Aid from Government

Grants-in-Aid from Government are as follows:

1. General Purpose, Maintenance and Development Fund

General purpose fund is utilized for meeting expenditure on traditional functions and establishment expenses.

Maintenance fund is utilized for maintaining assets of Panchayats including those transferred as part of decentralization. Maintenance fund is of two categories — one for the maintenance of roads and other for maintenance of assets.

Development fund is meant for the development purposes. It is of three categories, viz., General Sector, Special Component Plan and Tribal Sub Plan.

2. Grants-in-Aid for Implementing Schemes

(a) *Plan Schemes* — Plan schemes include Centrally Sponsored Schemes and State Sponsored Schemes have been transferred to Panchayats for implementation. The guidelines are formulated by the Central or State Governments and the role of Panchayat is limited to agency function i.e., deciding the location or beneficiary and executing the scheme.
(b) *Non Plan Schemes* — In addition to the Plan Schemes, grant-in-aid for implementing specific programmes under non-plan, particularly welfare pension are also given to Panchayats, *viz.*

(i) General education,
(ii) Medical and public health,
(iii) Labour and employment,
(iv) Welfare of SC/ST/OBC/Minority,
(v) Social Security and Welfare, and
(vi) Crop husbandry.

Loans: Panchayat can avail loans from financial institutions as per the Kerala State Local Authorities Loan Act (1963).

Table 3.15: Income and Expenditure Details for the Year 2010-11

Opening Balance as on 01.04.2010	Rs. 97,41,274
Receipts during 2010-11	Rs. 4,99,31,798
Total fund available during 2010-11	Rs. 5,96,73,072
Expenditure during 2010-11	Rs. 4,88,71,049
Closing balance as on 31.03.2011	Rs. 1,08,02,023

VIII. Functionaries and Facilities

All the Grama Panchayats are having their own building which can house the Panchayat Office, President's Chamber, Committee Room, Secretary's Room, Office Rooms, Record Room, Front Office etc. Office space for Kudumbasree and Mahatma Gandhi NREGA are also accommodated at the Panchayat office.

Human Resources at the Grama Panchayat

Grama Panchayats had their own staff. The staff creation is done by government. The terms and conditions are at par with government staff. But they are paid for by the Panchayat from their own resources as well as General Purpose funds from Government.

The Grama Panchayat is having the following staff:

Secretary	: 1
Junior Superintendent	: 1
Upper Division Clerks	: 3
Lower Division Clerks	: 3
Peon	: 1

With the introduction of the new functions to the Panchayat, Government had transferred institutions and offices along with staff to the Panchayat. The major problem faced was in the field of engineers, and to overcome the same a separate engineering wing for Local Self Government was established and now all Grama Panchayat have Overseers and two Grama Panchayats share one Assistant Engineer. The MGNREGA wing is having a separate Data Entry Operator-cum-Accountant and an Engineer on contract basis.

Photograph 3.10: The Secretary

Grama Panchayat have full managerial and part disciplinary control over the staff. They can assign any work to the transferred staff in area related to them. They can review their performance and give required directions. They are empowered to impose minor penalties.

The salaries of staff transferred continue to be paid by the Government, to ease the Panchayat from unnecessary burdening. Panchayat is engaging daily wage driver to operate their vehicle.

The Panchayat is equipped with furniture, electricity and phone connection (separate connection to the President, Secretary and office). The Grama Panchayat is having a good vehicle (Mahindra Xylo) for the Panchayat authorities to travel inside the Panchayat and also for attending meetings at the district headquarters. The Panchayat is having good computer facilities and internet connection. Separate computer and internet facilities are available for Kudumbasree office at Grama Panchayat and Mahatma Gandhi NREGS.

With the devolution of new functions the principle of work and workers going together was transferred to the Panchayats as shown in Table 3.16.

IX. Problems in Governance

A. Problems of Governance at the Panchayat Level

Even though development functionaries from agriculture, animal husbandry, rural development, social welfare, primary education, dairy, Scheduled Caste and Scheduled Tribe Development, health service up to PHC were transferred to the Grama Panchayat, actual transfer is not effected due to departmentalism prevails among these functionaries and also

Table 3.16: Officials Transferred from the Department

Department	*Office and Staff Transferred*
Agriculture	Agricultural Officer and auxiliary posts
Animal Husbandry	Officers and staff of Veterinary Sub-Centre, Veterinary Dispensary/Hospital and ICDP Sub Centres
Fisheries	Fisheries Sub-Inspector
Rural Development	Two Village Extension Officers including one Lady VEO
Social Welfare	Officers and staff of Day Care Centre and Anganwadis (ICDS Supervisor, Anganwadi worker/helper, etc.)
SC Development	Officers and staff of Balawadis, Balawadi-cum-feeding centres
ST Department	Officers and staff of Balawadis, Balawadi-cum-feeding centres
Health Services (Allopathic)	Medical Officer and staff of PHC
Health Services (Homoeo)	Medical Officer and staff of PHC
Health Services (ISM)	Medical Officer and staff of PHC
General Education	Head Masters, Teachers and other staff of Primary Schools
PWD/Irrigation	Asst. Engineer and auxiliary posts

the coition politics prevents the Panchayats to wield power over the functionaries given to the Panchayat.

Lack of proper training for planning and implementation of big amount by the Panchayats themselves (i.e., 40 per cent of the budget) is posing another problem.

Politically elected Panchayat members are not coming out of their political orbit for a broad based development perspective.

The pivot on which all the development activities in a Panchayat revolves is the effective functioning of Grama Sabha, which is seldom conducted on a proper way.

B. Problems of Elected Representatives

Since money and necessary powers were given to the Panchayats, the representatives of the Panchayat are answerable to the public. Since the demands of the public are very large and the resource available is scarce compared to the demand, the Panchayat often find it very difficult to satisfy the public.

Panchayat being a very small unit of administration and close to the people, the members are having close relation to the public and very often they have to attend the demands of those who are capable of putting their demand well and this ultimately leads to ignoring the demands of the weaker sections.

Planning in a micro arena is not as easy as one may think of. The expertise needed for planning may not be available in many cases and this will lead to some kind of adjustments in the name of planning.

50 per cent reservation and the system of rotating reserved wards lead to have almost all the members are elected for their first time. This inexperience also is an issue to be addressed through good training.

C. Problems faced by Women Representatives

From the inception of the new Panchayati Raj Act one-third of the seats were reserved for women and from the last election held in October 2010 onwards 50 per cent seats are reserved for them. The new system demands more participation from the side of women to Panchayat and thereby to politics.

Since the reserved seats are rotating every time those women who got elected may not usually get a second term.

This is causing the entry of more and more new women representatives who have very little knowledge in running a Panchayat. In the long run this certainly will generate a large pool of women in Panchayat activities but for the beginning this will cause certain problems.

In real terms what happens in a Panchayat is that whenever a Ward is reserved for women the political parties tend to prefer only members from their own families as candidates may be out of fear for their changing loyalties or because of non-availability of suitable candidates. A woman got candidature mainly because the seat is reserved, and hence there would be a potential male candidate who could not contest because of the reservation and it happens that he will pull the strings.

When a woman became member of a Panchayat, she is supposed to do all the activities of a member such as attending the Panchayat, attending the committees, attending functions arranged by them, attend the activities of political parties, attend social functions, look after the welfare of women at large, etc. More than that being a woman they had to look after the family business more than that of a male counterpart. So the burden of a woman member is three-fold compared to her male counterpart, i.e., the burden of Panchayat activities, burden of domestic duties and also the controls from political parties.

The woman members are also under the strict vigilance of the political parties who had field them for election. In many cases they were not even permitted to speak to outsiders on behalf of the Panchayat. Whenever someone visit a Panchayat, a male member who might have been President but because of the reservation will come out and speak on behalf of the Panchayat. In many cases this role is done by the Vice President.

D. Party Politics in Panchayat

A good Panchayat system does not need a strong party system because the activities of the Panchayat are non-political or apolitical in nature. But in Kerala elections to the Panchayats are fought on political lines and these results in creating problems to the day-to-day functions of a Panchayat.

One argument for the role of political parties and Panchayats run on political lines is that some kind of a broad political vision and guidance is readily available in a politically driven Panchayat, whereas in a non-political system the Panchayat Committee may not get a perspective plan for a broadbased development.

When the members are elected on political lines the arguments put forward by the members of opposition get little attention from the ruling parties.

E. Corruption in Governance

Transparency is maintained at every stages of administration. Decisions were taken based on norms and criteria evolved on the basis of social consensus and the rationale behind each decision has to be made public. There should be freedom to the people to know every detail of how money is going to be spent, before a scheme is taken up; and how it was spent, after completion. The procedures are made people friendly.

To avoid corruption and favouritism, the system of front office is introduced in the Panchayat, whereby people who approach the Panchayat can straightaway contact the officer in-charge of it and make request for some service and get receipt for it and through the front office they can get their demands satisfied in the specified time limit.

Absolute right to information is there in the system. Citizen's Charter was published indicating the entitlements of citizens' *vis-à-vis* a Local Government with respect to the quality and standards of various services provided by that Local Government.

X. Technology and Culture

Kerala is said to be neither urban nor rural — rather a "RURBAN" continuum. It is a continuum of residential areas. Most of the modern technologies available in an urban area are available at the Panchayat also.

All major mobile phone companies operate in the Panchayat, viz., Aircel, Airtel, BSNL, MDS, Reliance, Tata, Videocon, Vodafone, Uninor, etc. 82 per cent of the people above the age of 15 are using mobile phones.

Private vehicles like cars and two wheelers are in possession by 72 per cent families. Major cable TV operators also functions here. Computer usage is common among the people. Akshaya (an initiative of State Government) e-centre is helping them to learn and use computer. 40 per cent houses and 90 per cent offices are having computers. Internet connection is 21 per cent and 80 per cent respectively.

Family/Social Functions

The major family/social functions are marriage, funeral, birthday, house warming, introduction to letters, etc. Family functions of all communities are being attended mainly by relatives, friends and neighbours. These functions are a get-together for the family members and relatives.

Marriages are a function attended by hundreds of people mainly relatives. Only invited persons will attend the function, which will be conducted on some auspicious days, and for Hindus the ceremony is held in the presence of elders and for Christians and Muslims it will be solemnised by priests. Marriages are mainly conducted in community halls or temples and a feast will be followed. It is becoming an expensive function these days, especially for the family of the bridegroom.

Funerals are also arranged by the family members with the assistance of community (caste) leaders. It will be done at the premises of their houses if the family is having sufficient land. Generally, it will be done at the burial ground. Akathethara Panchayat is having two burial grounds — one for the general public and other for the caste Hindus. Muslims and Christians will do it at the mosque/church itself. The funeral functions also will be followed by prayers and a feast.

Public/Political Functions

Public functions are mainly organised by the political, social, religious or caste organisations. Some youth organisations are also organising it. It may be in the nature of meetings, rallies, conventions, etc., to give some message to the people or acts as a pressure tactics.

Major political parties like CPI (M), Congress (I), BJP, Muslim League and CPI are arranging their own functions for political causes. Political parties are also conducting some party functions.

Festivals

Festivals are mainly religious in nature and some social festivals are also celebrated here. Hindus forms a majority in this Panchayat and hence most of the festivals celebrated are related to the temples of this area. Though the festivals are being conducted by temples, every people in the Panchayat are enjoying it. These festivals also act as an opportunity for the local people for a get together.

Social Behaviour and Public Life

Generally the people are leading a peaceful life. People used to help others in need. No communal issues occurred here.

The major social issue faced by the people here is the rise in number of people using liquor. It is increasing day by day. Using liquor is not considered as a bad habit — at least among the new generation. The habit of using liquor on functions is also spreading.

The system of dowry is another social evil faced by the people. Nobody is actually coming out against it. People at large consider girl child as a burden, because of the dowry system.

Jagratha Samithy

Conflicts in society and its redressal have many ways — formal and informal. Formal means are police, court, etc., and informal means are mediation by elders, Panchayat members, political leaders, Community leaders, Caste leaders, Churches and NGOs. For settling such disputes and Jagratha Samithy is there to ensure smooth living.

Akathethara Panchayat is having a Jagratha Samithy at Panchayat level as well as at ward levels. The Jagratha Samithy at Panchayat level is having the following members.

- Panchayat President,
- Circle Inspector of Police,
- Lady Advocate,

Photograph 3.11: Session of Jagratha Samithy

- ICDS Supervisor,
- Lady Doctor,
- CDS Chairperson,
- Chairman, Welfare Standing Committee, and
- Lady Member of Panchayat.

XI. Economic Trends

Land Ownership

Kerala is probably the only State in India where land reforms were implemented in letter and spirit. In the case of Akathethara itself, formerly the entire land was under the ownership of the Emoor Devaswom. With the land reforms the entire land was given to the people lived there. No kind of alienation of land exists here.

Migration

Migration to other areas including foreign countries is a

common phenomenon in Kerala and Akathethara is no exception. A sizable number of people had migrated from here in search of better living and job and not in search of a menial job. Most of this migration was made by the middle class and upper middle class.

Concluding Remarks

Akathethara is a cross-section of Grama Panchayats in Kerala. Geographically the State is divided into three regions, viz., coastal, midland and highland. Majority of the population is concentrated in the coastal areas. Most of the towns/cities also are there. The main traditional occupation of the people living in coastal areas is directly linked to the sea and inland waterbodies, like fishing, coir, etc., and paddy cultivation. Midland represents the agricultural region of Kerala. Paddy is the main cultivation, but economic crops like rubber is now gaining prominence here. Spices are also grown here. The high land which is closer to the Western Ghats is famous for its spices and tea plantations. Coconut is cultivated in the coastal areas and midlands.

Akathethara has the features of midland as well as high land. It is closer to the Western Ghats. Like most of the rural areas of Kerala is semi-urban. Kerala is a land where there is no clear distinction between urban and rural areas. The rural concept prevails in other parts of India is quite absent in Kerala. It has no isolated Grama/Village Panchayats. The entire Kerala is a continuation of rural and urban areas and hence the qualities of either can be seen everywhere. It is rather "rurban" in nature, i.e., neither rural nor urban.

Akathethara cannot claim to represent the village Panchayat system of any other State in India. Since Kerala is peculiar in many ways and different from the basic characteristics of rural India, this is only a representative Panchayat of Kerala.

The peculiarities of Kerala are many which keep it stand aloof from other areas of India. It is called "Gods own country". It has the highest level of literacy among Indian States, lowest Infant Mortality Rate in India. It has a moderate tropical climate, abundant in water resources and rain, higher density of population, Quality of Life Index, immigration to foreign nations, etc. In a way Kerala keeps high standards of living comparable to the advanced countries without the so-called economic development. The Kerala model of development is well appreciated all over the world and Dr. Amartya Sen often quotes it as an example for the developing countries.

Since time immemorial Kerala or the Malabar Coast had close trade relations with the West and East. Actually the Western geographical enquiries started to find a way to the Malabar Coast for collecting spices. Naturally all the western explorers came here for trade. Before that the Arabs, Greeks, Romans and Egyptians had very strong trade relations with the then Kingdoms of Kerala.

The initiatives taken by Akathethara Grama Panchayat were fully supported by the line departments of the State government in many ways. When the Panchayat started Green the Gap programme the forest department helped them in selection of plants, imparting ways to preserve them and they even supplied plants free of cost. The Panchayat initiated the solid waste management system with the support of the Sanitation Mission at the State level. Watershed development projects were supported by the Agriculture and Soil Conservation Departments. Health, education, SC development, Animal Husbandry and all other development departments supported the initiatives taken by the Panchayat.

The overall performance of the Panchayat is well appreciated by Government at several times. This was made possible by the efforts taken by the elected representatives. Regardless of the political background, once elected they all come together and worked for the well-being of the entire Panchayat. Another important reason for their success lies in ensuring the participation of the local people in all the public forums like Grama Sabha, Jagratha Samithi, etc., any development programme can succeed only if it ensures the participation of the people. The people in this Panchayat are actively participating in the initiatives taken by the Panchayat.

NOTES

Akathethara Grama Panchayat, Powravakasha Rekha (Citizen's Charter) (Palakkad: Akathethara Grama Panchayat, 2009).

Government of Kerala, Kerala Panchayats Act, (1960) (Trivandrum: Government of Kerala, 1970).

Government of Kerala, Kerala Panchayat Manual (Trivandrum: Government of Kerala, 1977).

Government of Kerala, Kerala Panchayati Raj Act 1994 (Trivandrum: Government of Kerala, 2002).

Government of Kerala, Kerala Panchayati Raj — Registration of Electors Rules (Trivandrum: Government of Kerala, 1994).

Kerala State Land Use Board, Land Resources of Kerala (Trivandrum: Kerala State Land Use Board, 1995).

Thomas Issac, Local Democracy and Development: People's Campaign for Decentralised Planning in Kerala (New Delhi: Leftward Publishers, 2000).

Tax Revenue Records, Akathethara Grama Panchayat.

Work Register, Akathethara Grama Panchayat.

Index